GW01339901

LEGENDS OF FLIGHT

AIRBUS A300/310

A Legends of Flight Illustrated History

WOLFGANG BORGMANN

Schiffer Military
4880 Lower Valley Road Atglen, PA 19310

Copyright © 2021 by Schiffer Publishing, Ltd.

Originally published as *Die Flugzeugstars Airbus A300* by Motorbuch Verlag, Stuttgart © 2018 Motorbuch Verlag
Translated from the German by David Johnston

Library of Congress Control Number: 2020943433

All rights reserved. No part of this work may be reproduced or used in any form or by any means—graphic, electronic, or mechanical, including photocopying or information storage and retrieval systems—without written permission from the publisher.

The scanning, uploading, and distribution of this book or any part thereof via the Internet or any other means without the permission of the publisher is illegal and punishable by law. Please purchase only authorized editions and do not participate in or encourage the electronic piracy of copyrighted materials.

"Schiffer Military" and the arrow logo are trademarks of Schiffer Publishing, Ltd.

Cover design by Molly Shields
Type set in DIN/Minion Pro/Brandon Grotesque/Axia

ISBN: 978-0-7643-6139-5
Printed in China

Published by Schiffer Publishing, Ltd.
4880 Lower Valley Road
Atglen, PA 19310
Phone: (610) 593-1777; Fax: (610) 593-2002
E-mail: Info@schifferbooks.com
Web: www.schifferbooks.com

For our complete selection of fine books on this and related subjects, please visit our website at www.schifferbooks.com. You may also write for a free catalog.

Schiffer Publishing's titles are available at special discounts for bulk purchases for sales promotions or premiums. Special editions, including personalized covers, corporate imprints, and excerpts, can be created in large quantities for special needs. For more information, contact the publisher.

We are always looking for people to write books on new and related subjects. If you have an idea for a book, please contact us at proposals@schifferbooks.com.

CONTENTS

006 FOREWORD

010 CHAPTER 1 THE AIRBUS PROGRAM A300 AND A310
HIGHLIGHTS, 1965–1988

029 CHAPTER 2 THE AIRBUS SYSTEM
MORE THAN JUST AN AIRCRAFT

032 CHAPTER 3 THE EUROPEAN DREAM
TOGETHER WE ARE STRONG
032 The Airbus as the Engine of Europe

042 CHAPTER 4 AIRBUS IN HAMBURG
THE EVENTFUL HISTORY OF THE HAMBURGER FLUGZEUGBAU
050 The Tentative New Beginning
052 The Forward-Swept Wing
054 In Search of Partners
054 Loss of Independence

057 CHAPTER 5 THE A300 STORY
FROM POLITICAL ISSUE TO AIRLINER
060 The A300 Loses Weight
061 Comfort Jet
065 Lufthansa and the A300
066 The Lufthansa Requirements
068 The ATLAS Group

071 CHAPTER 6 ALLOCATION OF A300B WORK SHARES IN SEPTEMBER 1970
071 In the Entire Project
071 Within Germany
071 Construction Breakdown
074 German Factories Involved in the A300B

076 CHAPTER 7 AFTER THE CONTRACTS ARE SIGNED
SPARE-PARTS SUPPLY AND TRAINING
076 Airspares
078 Aéroformation

080 CHAPTER 8 BREAKTHROUGH IN AMERICA
EVERY BEGINNING IS HARD
082 Eastern Airlines: The First American Customer
084 New Hope in Pan Am
084 Image in Danger
086 Canadian A310s

088 CHAPTER 9 THE A300 MODELS
088 A300B1: The Prototypes
092 A300B2: The First Production Model
092 Selection by the KSSU Consortium
095 Planned
095 A300B4: The Success Model
098 The Freighters: A Second Life
103 The Airbus Elbe Flugzeugwerke A300 and A310 Freighters

104	**CHAPTER 10 THE SECOND GENERATION**
104	Airbus A310
110	A310: The Lufthansa Jet
114	The Wager
116	A300-600: The Big Sister

122	**CHAPTER 11 LOGISTICAL CHALLENGE**
	ANSWERED BEFORE THE FIRST FLIGHT
122	Aero Spacelines 377SGT Super Guppy Turbine 201
129	Airbus A300-600ST Beluga
129	Airbus A330-743L Beluga XL
132	Specifications of the Airbus Transports

135	**CHAPTER 12 THE AIRBUSES IN DETAIL**
	SPECIFICATIONS
140	Engine Overview: Engine Options Offered by Airbus for the A300 and A310

142	**BIBLIOGRAPHY**

A Lufthansa A300B2 shows off its lines against the background of a fascinating mountain of clouds. *Lufthansa*

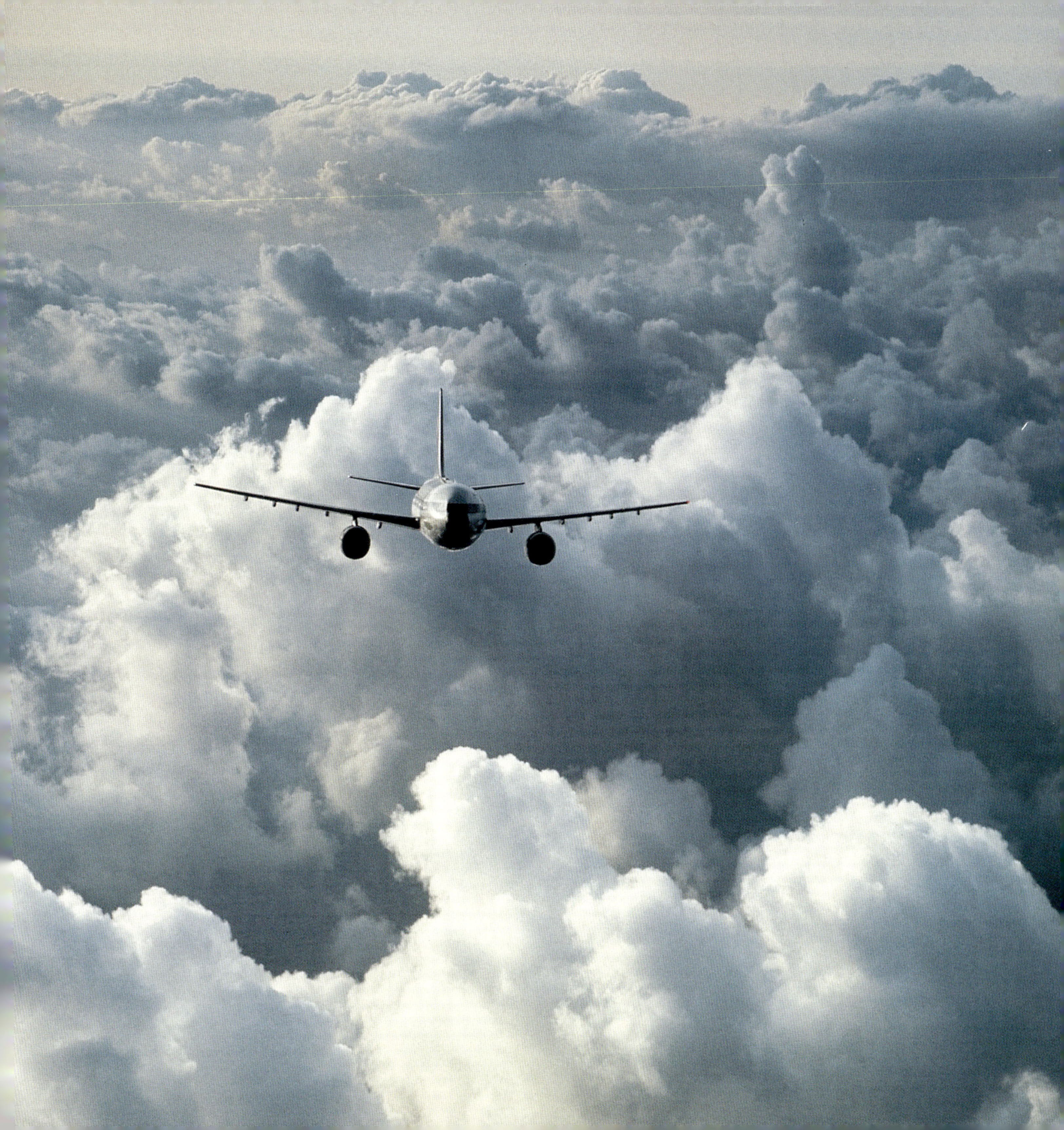

FOREWORD

This book not only examines the histories of the A300 and A310 aircraft types, it also concerns itself with the political and industrial aspects of the Airbus program. In particular it highlights their importance to the largest German Airbus facility at Hamburg-Finkenwerder. Without the forward-looking planning of its founding family, Blohm, which in the 1960s developed and built the HFB 320 Hansa Jet, the first jet-powered commercial aircraft produced in Germany, the Hamburg facility of the then Messerschmitt-Bölkow-Blohm GmbH (MBB) would not have had the required know-how to win out against the competing MBB facilities at Augsburg, Donauwörth, and Ottobrunn near Munich in southern Germany. As a result, the partners in southern Germany that dominated MBB had no other choice but to grant the facility on the Elbe with leadership of the German portion of the Airbus program. Together with the other production sites in northern Germany taking part in the Airbus program, at Varel, Nordenham (Einswarden), Lemwerder, and Bremen, plus the MBB facility in Stade, Hamburg, was one of five lined up like a string of pearls from west to east in the northern part of West Germany—and which with their work packages played a major role in the success of the A300 and A310.

Initially launched by the governments of France and Germany to promote the idea of European unity, in the 1970s and 1980s Airbus slowly but irresistibly began its journey toward its current

Pan Am, the tradition-rich airline founded in 1927, was the only American customer for the A310. *Airbus*

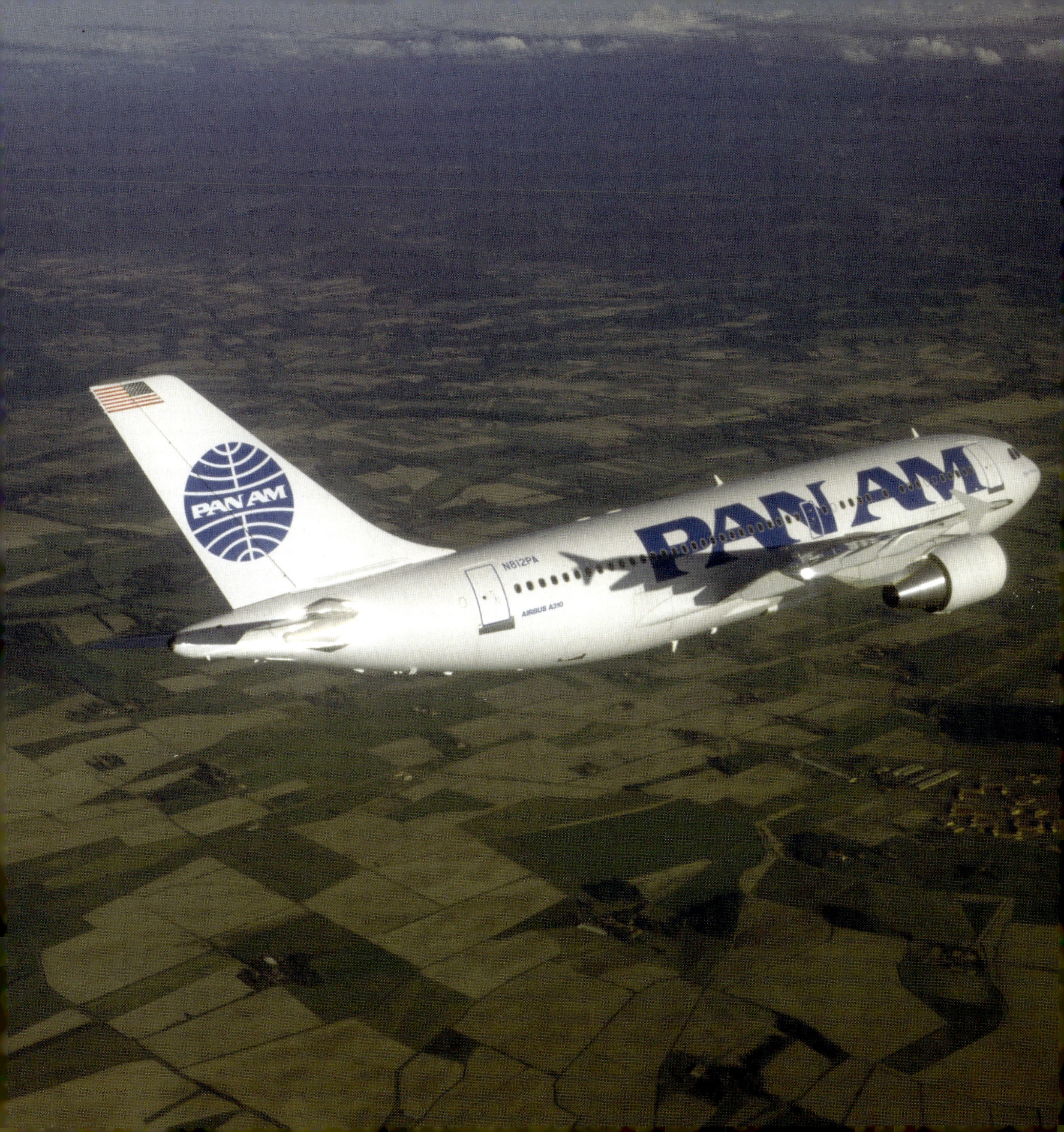
PAN AM
PAN AM
N812PA
AIRBUS A310

role as one of the two largest makers of commercial aircraft in the world. Ridiculed by its American competitors at first, despite all the national jealousies between the participating nations and the different work practices, languages, and mentalities, the Airbus managers held true to their dream of a pan-European aircraft maker. Its founding fathers deserve praise for having successfully defended the Airbus idea against the vehement resistance of its many doubters during the program's difficult initial years. Even the year and a half absence of new contracts in the mid-1970s could not divert them from their course. These challenging times may be forgotten in the face of the current sales boom, but it is extremely likely that had European civil aviation failed at that time, it would have fallen into a deep sleep instead of becoming what it is today a high-tech branch that functions as a driver of the economy and an employer with a promising future of tens of thousands of people in Europe, China, and the United States.

Wolfgang Borgmann
Oerlinghausen, summer 2018

An atmospheric sunset over an Eastern Airlines A300B4. Note the perfectly circular fuselage.

FOREWORD 9

CHAPTER 1
THE AIRBUS PROGRAM A300 AND A310
HIGHLIGHTS, 1965–1988

June 18, 1965
Ludwig Bölkow and Dr. Bernhard Weinhardt, then managing director of the Bölkow GmbH, meet with General André Puget, president of the French aircraft maker Sud Aviation, based in Toulouse, at the Paris Le Bourget air show to discuss construction of a German-French wide-body aircraft.

July 2, 1965
The West German aircraft makers Bölkow GmbH / Siebelwerke ATG GmbH, Dornier GmbH, Hamburger Flugzeugbau GmbH, and Vereinigte Flugtechnische Werke GmbH agree to begin detailed planning for a wide-body aircraft in cooperation with other European manufacturers.

August 1965
The "research bureau" moves into its office in the Deutsches Museum in Munich. Not far from the legendary Junkers Ju 52/3m on display there, the engineers plan the European aircraft of the future. The "Airbus Research Bureau" is led by Karl Frydag, who during the Second World War was head of the Central Committee for Aircraft Production in the Reich Ministry of Armaments and War Production, and director general of the Heinkel group.

October 22, 1965
Representatives of the European Airbus partners and delegates from ten European airlines meet in London to discuss the marketing possibilities of a wide-body jet produced by a pan-European cooperative effort. Conclusion: if the aircraft is designed for the global aviation market and not for a few national airlines, such as the D.H. 121 Trident or Vickers VC-10, the project has good chances of success. Airbus initially ignores the proposals made by the airlines.

November 1965
As a result of the London meeting, studies for an aircraft with 225 seats are initially pursued.

THE AIRBUS PROGRAM A300 AND A310   11

Along with Lufthansa, Swissair played a major part in the definition of the A310. This photo depicts an aircraft of the former Swiss airline in flight over the Swiss Alps. *ETH-Bibliothek Zurich, Swissair*

November 5, 1965
The German Airbus partners meet with members of the West German government in Bad Godesberg to discuss participation by the state in the high development costs. The estimated financial requirement for the German companies alone: 400 million deutsch marks.

December 3, 1965
The German Airbus Consortium is formed in Munich under the leadership of Karl Frydag.

December 1965
The British aircraft maker Hawker-Siddeley and the French partners Nord Aviation and Bréguet agree on the Airbus definition. Various project studies with the designations HBN 100 to 104 are investigated. One of them is for an aircraft with two passenger decks like the A380.

Winter 1965–1966
German minister for economics and technology Kurt Schmücker (Christian Democratic Union) reaches an agreement with British minister of aviation Roy Jenkins that the Federal Republic will bear 25 percent of the costs, while the two European partners France and Great Britain will share the remaining 75 percent.

March 1966
The federal German cabinet agrees to provide the Airbus program financial support on the proviso that Great Britain and France bear the major financial burdens.

May 1966
The ministers of France, Germany, and Great Britain involved in the Airbus program lay out what the new wide-boy aircraft is to look like as per the Ministries Outline Specification, without consulting potential customers. The step is met with incomprehension by the airlines worldwide.

June 13, 1966
Representatives of European airlines meet in Paris to formulate their expectations of the design and especially the profitability of the A300. None of these ideas are adopted by Airbus. This is followed by the public rejection of the A300 concept by British European Airways and Lufthansa.

September 8, 1966
At the Farnborough Airshow, politicians from all three partner nations—Germany, France, and Great Britain—consult on the implementation and financing of the Airbus program, which has still not been officially launched.

Summer 1967
- Roger Béteille of Sud Aviation is named the project's technical director and is based in the city of Toulouse. France assumes the leading role in the Airbus project.
- In June of the year the A300 definition specifies an aircraft capable of transporting a maximum of 298 passengers in a cabin 21 feet wide, with nine seats per row, over a maximum range of 1,926 miles, with a cruising speed of 574 mph.

September 4, 1967
- The Deutsche Airbus GmbH is established on the museum island in Munich with a share capital of just five million deutsch marks. It replaces the Airbus Research Bureau. Its members are Dornier, Hamburger Flugzeugbau, Messerschmitt Werke / Flugzeug-Union-Süd, Siebelwerke ATG, and VFW.
- Its managing directors: Dr. Bernhard Weinhardt, Karl Frydag, and Hans Wocke.
- Wocke, who was sent to Munich by the Hamburger Flugzeugbau GmbH, assumes the role of program director and acts as chairman of the board.

September 27, 1967

- Start of the concrete "project definition phase." In Bonn, the British minister of technology John Stonehouse, French transport minister Jean Chamant, and Klaus Schütz, state secretary in the Foreign Office in Bonn, sign a memorandum of understanding concerning development of the Airbus.
- It is agreed that the French and British partners will each bear 37.5 percent of the development and production costs, with Germany assuming the remaining 25 percent.
- At the same time, the aircraft is defined to have a maximum seating capacity of 290 passengers and a range of 932 miles.
- At this early stage of the project, the European partners also agree on a fuselage diameter of 18.5 feet, which will remain unchanged when the aircraft enters production.
- Two RB 207 turbofan engines, developed by Rolls-Royce for the project, are chosen as power plants for the project. Initially, therefore, the Airbus is a purely European product.

October 31, 1967

Felix Kracht is appointed to the executive board of the German Airbus GmbH to oversee production.

August 2, 1968

- At a meeting of ministers from the Airbus partner states in Paris, it is decided that the design studies currently being examined will be continued for another four months.
- The Airbus partners establish the supply organization Airbus International S.A., based in Paris under the leadership of Dr. Weinhardt.

1968–1969

The Airbus is now conceived with a maximum of 300 seats and is therefore given the type designation A300.

April 10, 1969

- The design of the A300B is reduced from a seating capacity of 300 to about 250.
- Its fuselage shrinks from 21 feet in diameter to 18.5 feet. Its length is reduced from 177 feet to 158.5 feet.
- The A300B is 27.5 tons lighter than the originally conceived A300.
- Rolls-Royce cancels the RB 207 engine program in favor of the RB 211. At first, Airbus has no other power plant available for the A300B.
- The British government withdraws its promise of financing and officially withdraws from the Airbus program.
- The fusion of Nord Aviation, Sereb, and Sud Aviation results in the creation of the French Société Nationale Industrielle Aérospatiale (SNIAS) under the leadership of Henri Ziegler. This makes a substantial contribution in allowing the French and German governments to continue the Airbus project even without the British partner.

May 12, 1969

VFW and Fokker merge to form a company based in Dusseldorf. Each partner provides half the capital funds of 100 million deutsch marks.

May 29, 1969

- The German federal government seizes the opportunity and takes over the British share of the Airbus project, which is now solely in German-French hands.
- Federal minister of economic affairs Karl Schiller (Social Democratic Party) and the French transportation minister Jean Chamant sign the agreement between the German and French governments concerning the development and construction of the European Airbus A300B in a mockup of the A300B cockpit at the Aérosalon at Paris Le Bourget.

- The British aircraft maker Hawker-Siddeley Aviation joins the Airbus program, at its own risk and without support from the British government, as project partner for wing manufacture. In the spirit of the European Union, the German government provides Hawker-Siddeley with a loan covering 50 percent of the costs of setting up production facilities.
- The Rolls-Royce RB 211-61 is now offered to the airlines as the standard power plant.
- At its plant in Bremen, VFW-Fokker takes over the manufacture of all movable wing components, such as slats and flaps.

Spring 1970
In addition to the British Rolls-Royce RB 211, Airbus now also offers the American General Electric CF6-6 engine as an alternative power plant.

March 1970
Franz Josef Strauß, chairman of the Bavarian Christian Social Union and later minister-president, takes over as chairman of the supervisory board of German Airbus GmbH. A private pilot, Strauß subsequently becomes a driving force behind the Airbus project and defends it against political and economic naysayers in German and Europe.

September 1970
Dornier leaves the loss-making Airbus program because of the risk associated with a financial investment of ten million deutsch marks.

December 18, 1970
- The Deutsche Airbus GmbH and Aérospatiale establish Airbus Industrie as an economic-interest grouping, or *groupement d'interet economique* in French. The agreement is signed by Franz Josef Strauß for the German side and Henri Ziegler for France. Airbus Industrie can at any time fall back on a total workforce of 120,000 employees of its European partners.
- Franz Josef Strauß is chosen to be chairman of the board of Airbus Industrie.
- In the following years, Ziegler as managing director and Strauß are guarantors for the continuation of the Airbus project, which they successfully defend against all political and economic opposition.
- The inaugural meeting also names the following technical directors, whose names are inextricably linked to the success of Airbus: Roger Béteille (technology and coordination), Felix Kracht (production), Hugo Friedrich Krambeck (administration and finance), and Didier Godechot (sales).
- Roger Béteille pushes through English as the working language of the Airbus consortium, and the use of the Anglo-American system of measurement as standard in global aviation.

December 28, 1970
The Dutch-German Fokker-VFW Flugzeugwerke invests in Airbus as an associate partner.

Spring 1971
The A300B is henceforth offered exclusively with the General Electric CF6-6 engine—from 1972 onward, the CF6-50 version. This makes it possible for customers of the Boeing 747-200, McDonnell Douglas DC-10, and Airbus A300B to use the same power plants in all three types.

November 3, 1971
Air France places a binding order for six A300Bs and ten options, becoming the first airline worldwide to do so.

June 23, 1972
The Spanish company CASA becomes a member of Airbus Industrie.

September 28, 1972
Rollout of the A300B1 prototype at Toulouse

One of the first official model photos of the A300B released by the manufacturer. Apart from its basic outlines, it bears little resemblance to the aircraft as actually built. *Hamburger Flugzeugbau GmbH*

LEFT The first flight crew posing in front of the A300B1 after their successful flight on October 28, 1972. *Airbus*

OPPOSITE Air France was the first customer for the A300B, with an order for six examples on November 3, 1971. Air France established the trend of painting the aircraft's fuselage white, which continues to this day. *Air France*

October 28, 1972
First flight! With chief test pilot Max Fischl at the controls, the crew, consisting of Pierre Canell, Romeo Zinzoni, Bernard Ziegler, and flight engineer Günther Scherer of Bremen, lifts off on the 1.25-hour maiden flight of the A300B1 registered as F-WUAB.

February 5, 1973
Maiden flight by the second A300B1 test aircraft, with the registration F-WUAC.

June 29, 1973
Maiden flight by the third test aircraft, with the registration F-WUAD—the first A300B2 to fly.

October 1973
Three A300Bs take off from Toulouse on a global sales tour, which consists of visits to potential airline customers in eighteen countries on four continents.

November 20, 1973
The A300B2 F-WUAA completes the quartet of aircraft used for type certification.

March 15, 1974
The A300B2 becomes the first type ever to receive its German and French type certifications simultaneously. Airbus completes 1,585 flying hours with the four aircraft used for certification.

May 23, 1974
An A300B2-100 of launch customer Air France takes off from Paris on the first scheduled flight by the type. Destination of the premier flight by the Airbus registered F-BVGA is London-Heathrow.

May 30, 1974
The A300B2 is certified by the American regulatory body FAA.

September 1974
With an order for four A300B4s and two options, Korean Air Lines becomes the first customer for this developed extended-range version of the A300B2 base model. This was also the first order from a non-European airline.

THE AIRBUS PROGRAM A300 AND A310   17

18 AIRBUS A300/310

OPPOSITE While on a test flight, this A300B2 of Air Siam landed at the Hamburg-Fuhlsbüttel airport and was parked in front of its then-current freight building for press photos. *MBB*

RIGHT A300B2/B4 fuselages during assembly in the MBB factory in Hamburg. The components shown in this photo were produced for aircraft that Airbus delivered to the French airline Air Inter, Korean Air Lines of South Korea, and TEA of Belgium in 1975. *MBB*

September 30, 1974
The A300B2 is certified for category 3 instrument landings.

October 21, 1974
The short-lived Thai airway Air Siam becomes the second airline in the world to use the A300B2 on its route network. The first flight is from Bangkok to Hong Kong.

December 26, 1974
Maiden flight by an A300B4 with extended range and higher takeoff weight

1975
Bernard Lathière takes over leadership of Airbus Industrie from Henri Ziegler.

June 25, 1975
Lufthansa becomes an Airbus customer and signs a sales contract for three A300B2s plus options for nine more.

December 1975
- An eighteen-month slack period begins, which will go down in Airbus history as the "black period." Production is perforce reduced to 0.5 aircraft per month. By comparison, in 2017, Airbus delivered 718 aircraft—sixty per month! Nevertheless, at Toulouse there is a row of unsold aircraft, so-called white tails, which were produced to stock.
- The Airbus crisis brings together critics calling for the termination of the program. Only the vehement defense of the program by Airbus managing director Roger Béteille, Bernard Lathière, and Felix Kracht saves Airbus from closure.

February 2, 1976
Lufthansa takes delivery of its first brand-new A300B2-100 with the registration D-AIAA and baptizes it with the name Garmisch-Partenkirchen.

20 AIRBUS A300/310

Final assembly of the first Lufthansa A300B2 at Toulouse. *Lufthansa*

Formal handover of the first Lufthansa A300B2, with the registration D-AIAA, at Hamburg-Finkenwerder on February 9, 1976. In the background can be seen the tail of the second A300B4, destined for Germanair. *Lufthansa*

May 1977
A contract from Thai Airways International for up to four A300B4s ends the biggest Airbus crisis to date.

December 30, 1977
Scandinavian Airlines becomes the first customer for the A300B2 with Pratt & Whitney JT9D engines.

July 6, 1978
The A310 program is launched.

January 1, 1979
British Aerospace officially becomes a member of Airbus Industrie and contributes 20 percent to the A310 program, whose wings it designs and builds. The production of A300 wings, which BA built as an external partner, continues.

April 2, 1979
Acting jointly for the first time, Lufthansa and Swissair place the first order for the A310, in whose development their technical departments played a major role, as launch customers. The contract from Swissair specifies ten aircraft, while Lufthansa places a firm order for twenty-five A310s with options for twenty-five more.

May 2, 1979
Belgian Belairbus joins the Airbus A310 program.

October 3, 1979
The Spanish airline Iberia becomes the first airline to order the A300B4 with Pratt & Whitney JT9D engines.

March 21, 1980
Delivery of the one hundredth Airbus

February 16, 1982
Rollout of the A310-221 prototype F-WZLH with the paint schemes of its first two customers. The left half of the fuselage is in Lufthansa colors, while the right side is painted in Swissair colors. After completion of test flights, the aircraft is delivered to Swissair in March 1984 as HB-IPE. Other operators include Air Liberté and Federal Express before the A310 is retired in May 2015 and is parked at the American aircraft boneyard at Victorville.

April 3, 1982
Maiden flight by the A310-200, the second Airbus type, ten years after the A300B1

September 1982
The A310 test flights not only confirm its promising performance figures but reveal superior values. The A310 can fly about 2,000 feet higher than expected, and its economical cruise is Mach 0.81 instead of the Mach 0.79 promised in the sales brochures.

March 1983
The regulatory bodies simultaneously award the French and German type certifications for the A310.

March 29, 1983
Simultaneous handover of the first A310s to launch customers Lufthansa and Swissair

April 12, 1983
The A310 begins scheduled services with launch customers Lufthansa and Swissair.

July 8, 1983
Maiden flight by the A300-600 prototype. The third Airbus model offered for sale shares various components with the A310; for example, its cockpit and aerodynamically optimized aft fuselage.

The A300B4-120 shown here made its first flight on January 13, 1981, and was delivered to Iberia with the registration EC-DLE. *MBB*

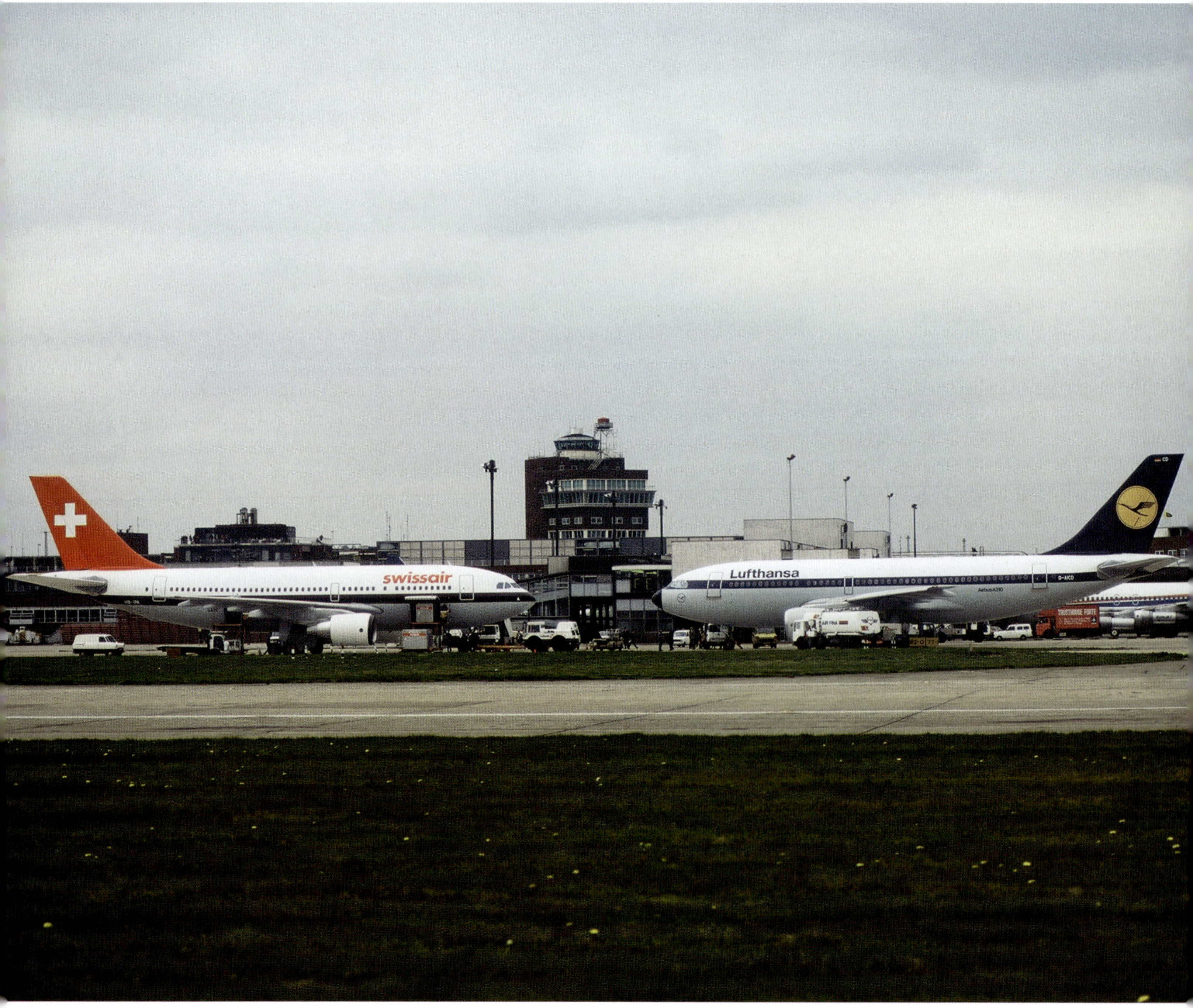
swissair
Lufthansa
D-AICD

OPPOSITE Swissair and Lufthansa revealed their new A310s to an expert audience at London-Heathrow on April 14, 1983. *Arthur Kemsley / Lufthansa*

RIGHT The A300-600 adopted the then very advanced glass cockpit of the smaller A310. *Lufthansa*

September 14, 1983
Onboard the Airbus A300 test aircraft, for the first time a sidestick controller is tested to control the aircraft under real conditions. The testing, which lasts seventy-five flying hours, is used to evaluate this design for the A320.

April 1984
The A300-600 begins scheduled service with its first customer, American Airlines.

May 1984
Airbus celebrates the ten-year anniversary of the beginning of scheduled service by the A300B2.

July 8, 1985
First flight by the A310-300 long-range version

July 17, 1985
The Lufthansa supervisory board authorizes the ordering of A300-600s.

March 10, 1988
The A300-600R (R standing for range) with increased range is certified by the French (DGAC) and Germans (LBA).

March 28, 1988
The A300-600 is certified by the FAA.

May 10, 1988
The A300-600R enters service with American Airlines.

June 24, 1988
Interflug, the national airline of East Germany, orders three A310-300s, becoming the first Eastern Bloc airline to order an Airbus. At the same time, it signs a contract with Lufthansa for maintenance and overhaul of the aircraft. From June 1989 onward, Interflug receives support from Lufthansa when its brand-new jets are delivered. After the end of Interflug following German reunification, all three A310-300s are taken over by the Luftwaffe for use as VIP and transport aircraft. The aircraft coded 10+21 (ex-DDR-ABA) was subsequently used by members of the federal government on

state visits before, in June 2014, it is modified by Lufthansa Technik in Hamburg to become a zero-gravity aircraft for weightlessness tests and since then has been in use by the French Novespace.

The former DDR-ABB also flew with the Luftwaffe as a VIP aircraft with the name Theodor Heuss, before being sold to Iran in 2011. There it served as the sole aircraft of Tehran Airlines. Finally, DDR-ABC was delivered to the Luftwaffe as 10+23 and with the name Kurt Schumacher remained in service in the summer of 2018. Shortly before its handover to the Luftwaffe, the A310, then registered D-AOAC, was involved in a serious incident at Moscow's Sheremetyevo airport. During a go-around the crew tried to fly the aircraft manually, but the autopilot was still engaged, resulting in three extreme, almost vertical climbs, each ending in a stall and dive. After the crew recognized its error, it was able to land the aircraft with its frightened passengers safely at Moscow.

October 3, 1988
Franz Josef Strauß dies. Until his death, he held the position of Airbus chairman of the board.

November 17, 1988
The German Free Democratic Party politician and banker Dr. Hans Friedrichs succeeds Strauß on the Airbus supervisory board.

December 31, 1988
At year's end there are 234 Airbus A300B2/B4s, forty-eight A300-600s, and 124 A310 airliners in service worldwide. The volume of orders since the start of sales activities in the early 1970s stands at 512 aircraft for sixty-four customers. Orders for twenty-one A300s and twenty-four A310s are received in Toulouse in 1988 alone. By that day, the global Airbus fleet had transported about 5.7 million passengers since the first scheduled flight on May 23, 1974, with an average technical dispatch reliability of 98.4 percent.

The A310-300 was the first Western airliner flown by the East German airline Interflug. *Airbus*

28　AIRBUS A300/310

The airline formed as TOA Domestic Airlines in 1964 was an early Airbus customer and operated thirty-nine A300B2/B4 and A300-600 aircraft (*photo*) on its Japanese domestic routes. Following its merger with Japan Air Lines (JAL) in 2002, it was renamed Japan Air System and, in 2004, was completely taken over by JAL. *Airbus*

CHAPTER 2
THE AIRBUS SYSTEM
MORE THAN JUST AN AIRCRAFT

When the managers of the five largest German aircraft manufacturers—Bölkow GmbH / Siebelwerke ATG GmbH, Dornier GmbH, Hamburger Flugzeugbau GmbH, Messerschmitt Werke / Flugzeug-Union-Süd, and Vereinigte Flugtechnische Werke GmbH—decided on July 2, 1965, to begin detail planning for a wide-body aircraft as a European cooperative effort, they were not simply imagining the construction of just another commercial aircraft. Instead they planned an Airbus system, which completely redefined the entire functioning of transportation—including the trip to and from the airport. At the time it was believed that this was the only way that the predicted two-figure growth rate in air traffic by the year 1980 could be handled.

In principle, the planners for the first time created something on their drawing boards that has not come to fruition to the present day: the creation of a close network of various modes of transport, including air travel, whose services are well coordinated and thus considerably shorten travel times. The result based on this premise was the Airbus system, which optimized every phase of travel from the traveler's departure from his home to his arrival at his destination.

The same was true of air freight, which was already becoming of major importance.

The airliner of the Airbus system was conceived to carry 250 to 300 passengers in scheduled and charter services over distances of about 600 miles. The members of the German Airbus Consortium saw the greatest need for a large aircraft in European aviation on these short-haul routes. During the night hours, however, the Airbus was to transport air freight and mail between economic centers. To get from the inner cities to the airports quickly, the Airbus team envisaged a rapid transport system based on the then newly developed monorail, a system that MBB had turned into a reality at Disneyland in Anaheim, at the gates of Los Angeles. The handling of air passengers, however, was to take place in completely newly built underground rapid-transit and air terminals, which would be located directly beneath the Airbuses above. The air passengers would be taken by escalator to the waiting aircraft without detours. The first Airbus aircraft study envisaged a four-engined high-wing monoplane, at first glance resembling a Lockheed C-5 Galaxy, which could transport freight and baggage on the lower deck and passengers on

30 AIRBUS A300/310

the upper deck. Freight pallets and baggage would be loaded and unloaded just as smoothly as passengers, using elevators and underfloor conveyor belts installed in the terminal. The primary purpose of the Airbus system was to make short-range air travel, which was notoriously unprofitable, viable. In this system, aircraft could be dispatched quickly and make their money by carrying out as many flights per day as possible.

The planned development of the new Airbus commercial aircraft gave the five German partner companies the unique opportunity to set the course for this transport system of the future. But the goals were set too high, and in the years that followed, the Airbus program limited itself to a conventional aircraft design, whose stream of passengers would quickly have brought many European airports of the early 1970s to the limits of their capacity. And so the Airbus led not to the speeding up, but rather to the slowing down of travel in completely overcrowded terminals, whose check-in facilities were too small in size and in which the mountain of luggage from up to 300 arriving passengers caused chaos at the baggage carousels.

This is how the German Airbus Consortium envisaged the "Airbus System" in 1965. It combined high-speed train and air travel with short changeover times between the modes of transport and extremely short ground times for the aircraft, optimized to convey a large volume of passengers and freight.
Borgmann collection

As actually built, the Airbus had little in common with the initial concepts from the German Airbus partner. The photo captures the A300B1 taking off on its maiden flight. *Airbus*

CHAPTER 3
THE EUROPEAN DREAM
TOGETHER WE ARE STRONG

THE TIME WAS RIPE FOR A EUROPEAN AIRCRAFT. —Ludwig Bölkow

Following the motto "together we are strong," in the 1960s the western European aircraft makers acted together in order to challenge the American dominance that existed in the commercial sector of the aviation industry. No European aircraft producer and no nation was financially and organizationally in a position to manage on its own a project the size of the Airbus. The opportunity that existed could succeed only at the European level. In its founding years, therefore, the Airbus was both a political and economic key project of the slowly coalescing western Europe. On March 25, 1957, the six European states of Belgium, Germany, France, Italy, Luxembourg, and the Netherlands had established the European Economic Community (EEC) in Rome. The Treaty of Rome signed there is considered the birth hour of the European Union and already had as its objective the free movement of persons, goods, and services within its borders. The agricultural policy of the EEC member states, introduced in 1962, was the forerunner of a united European aviation industry. Another important date was July 1, 1968, when for the first time duty-free border-crossing trade between nations became possible. The result was the largest trade zone in the world, which now set about to achieve great things on the aviation policy plane.

THE AIRBUS AS THE ENGINE OF EUROPE

It is almost a miracle that the components of the first A300B immediately fit together so perfectly during their assembly. Five countries—Germany, France, Great Britain, Spain, and the Netherlands, with an equal number of languages and aircraft construction standards—were working together. This was the time before computer-generated aircraft designs, and so the countless parts of the A300B were still designed by hand on the designers' drawing boards. Prior to the start of the project, there was neither a standard pan-European designation of the assemblies nor a standardized measuring system. And so the continental European Airbus partners

THE EUROPEAN DREAM 33

After the successful conclusion of flight trials, the second A300B1 prototype, originally registered F-WUAC, was fitted with a passenger cabin and sold to the Belgian charter airline TEA as OO-TEF. *Airbus*

34 AIRBUS A300/310

THE EUROPEAN DREAM

OPPOSITE The Nord 2501 Noratlas (*behind*), which was built under license by the Hamburger Flugzeugbau GmbH (HFB), and the Hansa Jet, developed and built by HFB at Hamburg-Finkenwerder, both were products of pan-European cooperation. In addition to German companies, contractors in Great Britain and Spain also took part in production of the HFB 320. *HFB*

RIGHT This schematic construction breakdown of the A300B among partner companies of the Airbus consortium reflects the status of the program in February 1971. *MBB*

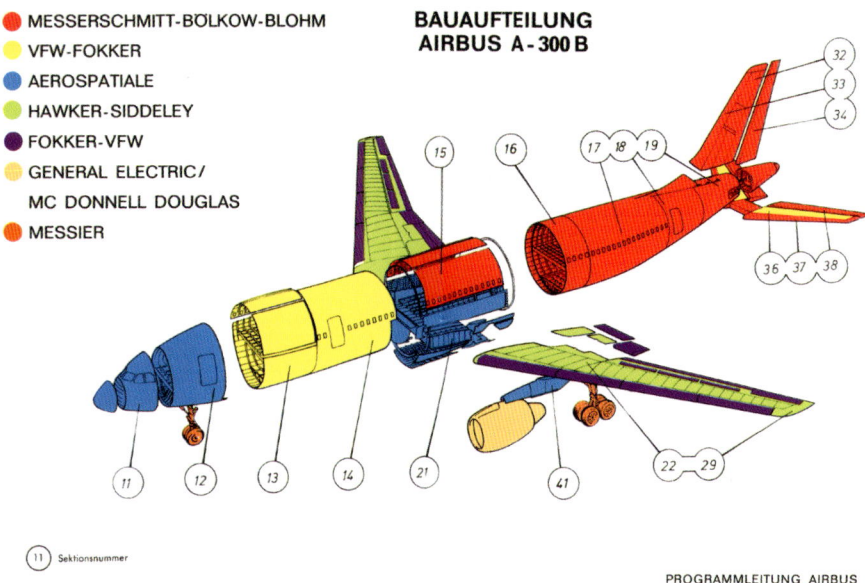

drew their plans in the metric system, while their British colleagues used the imperial system, with lengths in inches and feet. Many years before the introduction of the Euro, each of the five partner nations had its own national currency, with constantly changing rates of exchange. Very different mentalities and work styles in the various countries garnished this modern Babylon of future aircraft makers. It is thanks to Roger Béteille, who, as the first technical director of Airbus Industrie, created the principal conditions for the technical realization of this mammoth project. He decided that English should be the standard working language in the consortium, and that it would be the imperial system of measurements, not the metric system, that as the worldwide standard of aircraft construction would also form the basis of production at Airbus, supplemented by its own Airbus standards system.

The blending of economics and politics and the regard for national sensibilities led to an extremely complex Airbus company structure. On the basis of the government agreement between France and Germany of May 29, 1969, which the Netherlands joined in 1970, in the beginning it was not the Airbus aircraft makers who set the tone, but rather a governmental committee. The governments gave to this organ, which informed them of the technical, industrial, commercial, and financial progress of the program, leadership of the tasks that fell to them as part of the program. The governmental committee in turn formed an executive committee, which administered tasks assigned by the governmental committee and included a member of each government. Both committees could make use of state administrative bodies, which appeared under the title "administrative organ." The company groups Société Nationale Industrielle Aérospatiale (SNIAS) from France and the Deutsche Airbus GmbH, based in Hamburg, steered development and quantity production of the A300B via Airbus Industrie (AI), initially based in Paris and later Toulouse. AI was not, however, a conventional company in the form of stock company or limited-liability company (LLC), but rather an economic interest group, a *groupement d'interet economique* under French law.

In the background is the first section 15 upper-fuselage shell completed at Hamburg-Finkenwerder; in front of it is another section in the jig. The layout plan reveals that section 15 was in the center of the fuselage, above the wing center section. On the left of the photo, ongoing production of the C-160 Transall military transport for the Bundeswehr, which took place alongside production of A300B fuselage shell sections. *HFB*

How arduous the cooperation would be in practice due to political influence is shown by an anecdote from the year 1970 told by Professor Ernst Simon, who worked on the technical definition of the A300 on behalf of Lufthansa: "At one of the many meetings on this theme—it was in Paris and I regularly took part in them—the discussion, strictly following the diplomatic protocol of the many government representatives who were present, was making extraordinarily slow progress. First the French representative made his speech, in French naturally, then it was translated first into English by the interpreter and then into German. Each answer followed by way of the same procedure, and so on and so on. When it was my turn, I stood up and said that in the interest of efficiency I would like to shorten the procedure, and as I knew that all of those present spoke perfect English, I would use that language. By doing so I had probably disqualified myself from any diplomatic activity, but after that, the meeting proceeded much more quickly."

Airbus Industrie acted as the industry negotiating and contract partner to the committees formed by the associated governments, and concluded the main contract for development of the A300B. Until the official formation of Airbus Industrie on December 18, 1970, SNIAS also took over the role of official design organization. For its part, Airbus Industrie awarded subcontracts for the respective work shares, on the German side to Deutsche Airbus, which in turn commissioned the companies VFW-Fokker, Dornier, and MBB with work packages. After the departure of Dornier-Werke, to whom further financial participation seemed too risky, in September 1970 its work shares were assigned equally to the remaining project partners. The subcontract for development of the wings was signed on July 24, 1969, by Deutsche Airbus and SNIAS, with the British partner Hawker-Siddeley Aviation (HSA) as the executing company.

Financing of the A300B definition-and-development phase was arranged at a national level. The German share was secured by a conditionally repayable loan from the Federal Ministry for Economics in Bonn, with the German aviation industry putting up 10 percent of the necessary investment itself. Within the Messerschmitt-Bölkow-Blohm GmbH formed by merger in 1969, Hamburg-Finkenwerder was placed in charge of the Airbus project for the entire company. As the Hamburger Flugzeugbau GmbH, the site had amassed a great deal of experience on the national and European level during the development, production, sales, and spare-parts supply of the HFB 320 Hansa Jet. Ultimately, parts for the HFB 320 were also made by subcontractors in Spain and Great Britain, and a spare-parts organization operated twenty-four hours a day, 365 days a year, in support of customers on three continents. Nevertheless, the Airbus project was of an entirely different dimension, which quickly brought the Hamburg team to its limits. As an internal MBB paper from 1970 reveals, the plant management was then complaining about the absence of the necessary design experience and the insufficient number of qualified executives on the Elbe. MBB managing director Werner Blohm described in his memories of aircraft construction in Hamburg the complexity of the program and the associated dilemmas for MBB's Hamburg Division (UH) for which he was responsible: "The financial side of our work package was also very difficult. Here we were completely independent from Deutsche Airbus, which for its part worked according to guidelines from Airbus Industrie (AI). AI in turn had to take into account Boeing prices as a guideline. For us, therefore, there was no negotiating about prices." When MBB sharply reduced payments to UH in 1974 while leaving the work package unchanged, the Hamburg location went into the red, for which the southern German MBB partner blamed Werner Blohm personally—finally leading to his departure from the company in 1975.

LEFT September 1971: for the first time, an A300B component produced in Hamburg is loaded onto the Super Guppy special transport aircraft. *MBB*

OPPOSITE The first A300B1 prototype visiting Finkenwerder. *MBB*

Airbus Industrie continued to evolve with other partners and projects. CASA of Spain joined in 1971, while British Aerospace followed in the footsteps of Hawker-Siddeley in 1979 with wing production. In 1988, Aérospatiale of France and the MBB subsidiary Deutsche Airbus GmbH each held 37.9 percent of shares, British Aerospace in Great Britain 20 percent, and CASA 4.2 percent. Fokker of the Netherlands and Belairbus of Belgium were associate members. In 1980, the Messerschmitt-Bölkow-Blohm GmbH took over its northern German rival VFW-Fokker and also its Airbus work package—only to itself be swallowed up by Daimler-Benz on September 6, 1989. The Stuttgart automaker pooled its air and spaceflight holdings in DASA, which existed from 1989 until 2000. In the course of those eleven years the company retained its abbreviation, but to the joy of the printers of letterhead and visiting cards, it changed its name three times. The Deutschen Aerospace Aktiengesellschaft (*Aktiengesellschaft* meaning "stock company") followed the Daimler-Benz Aerospace Aktiengesellschaft, which after the merger of Chrysler and Daimler-Benz operated under the name DaimlerChrysler Aerospace Aktiengesellschaft.

In 2000, DASA merged with the French company Aérospatiale-Matra and the Spanish CASA to form the European air and space corporate group European Aeronautic Defense and Space Company, abbreviated EADS. Just a year later, the corporate group transferred the Airbus Industrie consortium, which had existed since 1970, into a fully integrated company called Airbus SAS, in which EADS held 80 percent of shares and the British air and space group BAE Systems 20 percent.

Since January 1, 2014, EADS, which was resident in the Netherlands, operated as the Airbus Group, under whose roof not only the civil airliners but also all types of air and space activities were combined. The company divided its activities into the branches Airbus Commercial, Airbus Defense, and Space and Airbus Helicopter. In the summer of 2018, the Hamburg factory was one of by then four final assembly centers in China, France, Germany, and the United States that assembled complete airliners.

THE EUROPEAN DREAM 39

40 AIRBUS A300/310

A300B OVERALL ORGANIZATION

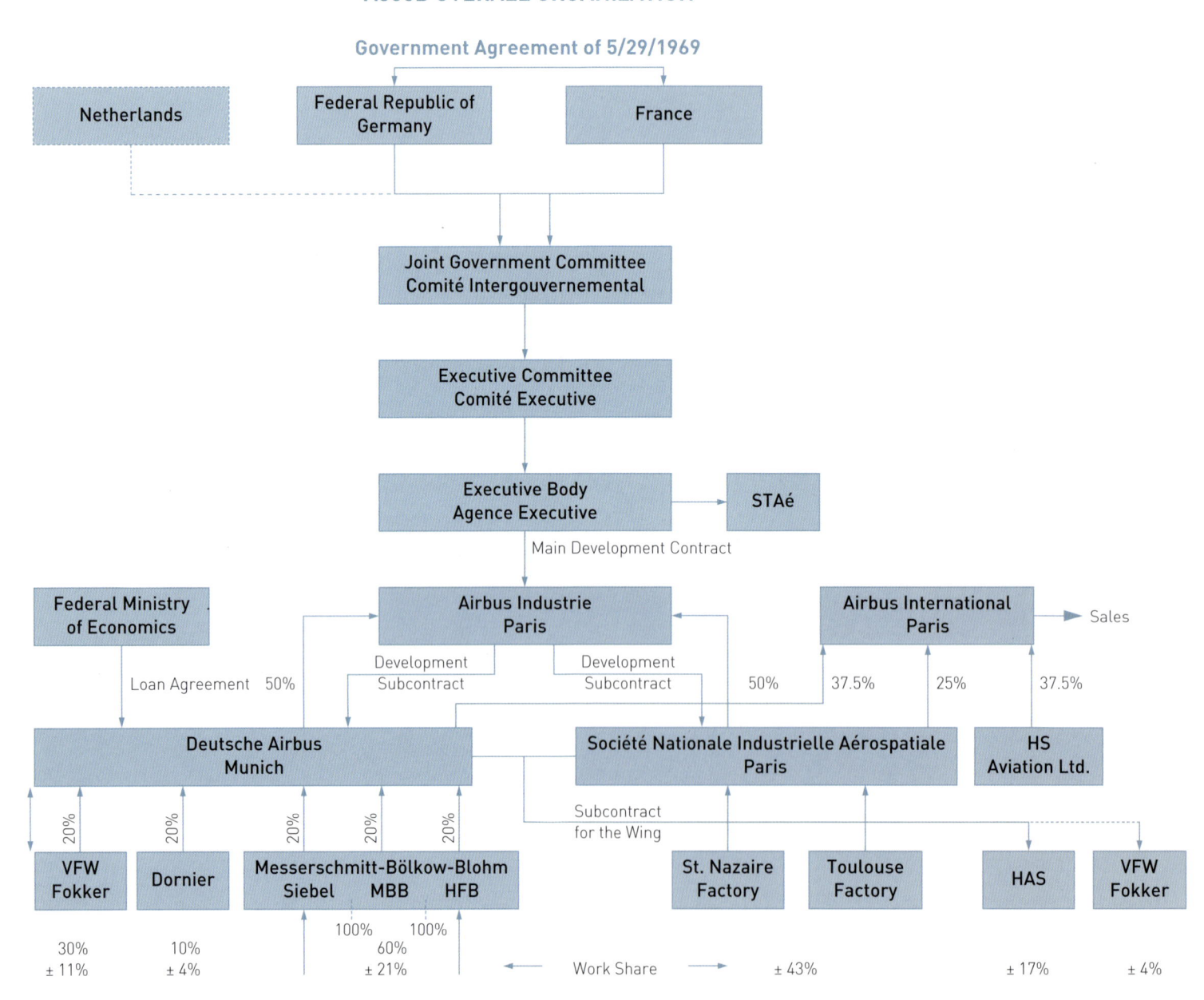

Government Agreement of 5/29/1969

- Netherlands
- Federal Republic of Germany
- France

↓

Joint Government Committee / Comité Intergouvernemental

↓

Executive Committee / Comité Executive

↓

Executive Body / Agence Executive → STAé

Main Development Contract

↓

Airbus Industrie Paris — **Airbus International Paris** → Sales

- Federal Ministry of Economics — Loan Agreement
- Development Subcontract 50% / 50%
- 37.5% / 25% / 37.5%

Deutsche Airbus Munich — **Société Nationale Industrielle Aérospatiale Paris** — **HS Aviation Ltd.**

Subcontract for the Wing

20%	20%	20%	20%	20%				
VFW Fokker	Dornier	Messerschmitt-Bölkow-Blohm Siebel / MBB / HFB			St. Nazaire Factory	Toulouse Factory	HAS	VFW Fokker
		100%	60%	100%				

Work Share:
± 11% ± 4% ± 21% ± 43% ± 17% ± 4%

30% / 10%

The Airbus program structure tree from 1969 reveals that it was not industry but the German and French governments that had the say in Airbus. *MBB*

Laker Airways of Great Britain ordered up to ten A300B4s from Airbus in 1979; however, it was able to take delivery of only three aircraft before its bankruptcy in 1982 (*above*). After the company ceased operating, two of these went to Air Jamaica, while another found a new home with Pakistan International (*below*). *MBB*

CHAPTER 4
AIRBUS IN HAMBURG
THE EVENTFUL HISTORY OF THE HAMBURGER FLUGZEUGBAU

WITHOUT THE HANSA JET, TODAY THERE WOULD BE NO AIRBUS PRODUCTION IN HAMBURG! —Werner Blohm, son of company founder and HFB manager

The history of the aircraft builder on the Elbe island of Finkenwerder has its roots in October of the year 1932. In the midst of the world economic crisis, brothers Rudolf and Walter Blohm, owners of the financially troubled Blohm & Voss shipyard, sought alternative employment opportunities for their employees as a result of the absence of contracts for the construction of new ships. Their shipyard empire had built the legendary fast steamer *Europa* for the Hapag-Lloyd shipping line, which on its maiden voyage had won the blue ribbon as the fastest ship on the North Atlantic. After its return to Hamburg, the *Europa* was fitted out with an aircraft catapult at the Blohm & Voss shipyard, from which a Junkers K46 carrying mail was launched long before the ship reached its destination—and thus reduced mail delivery times between the Old World and the New World by up to thirty hours. This was Rudolf and Walter Blohm's first indirect contact with aviation, before they established the Hamburger Flugzeugbau Gesellschaft mbH (HFB) in June 1933. In addition to Dipl.-Ing. Max P. Andrae, brother-in-law of the Blohm brothers, they appointed Robert Schröck as second managing director. The latter had previously worked for Bäumer Aero GmbH in Hamburg, which from 1924 to 1932 built small sporting aircraft at Hamburg-Fuhlsbüttel. Its most famous product was the Sausewind (*Sausewind* meaning "whirlwind"), which set several world speed and altitude records in its class.

Schröck was one of the very few early HFB employees with experience in building aircraft. And he had good contacts with the congenial twin brothers Walter and Siegfried Günter, whom Ernst Heinkel hired away from Bäumer Aero and brought to his aircraft company in Rostock. So it was obvious that Schröck first wanted to attract his former colleagues back to Hamburg. Even though he was unsuccessful, he returned to Hamburg with five other Heinkel engineers, who immediately began planning the first HFB aircraft type. The result of these efforts was the Ha 135, a small, two-seat, fabric-covered biplane trainer, which took off on its maiden flight from Hamburg-Fuhlsbüttel on April 28, 1934. The Fuhlsbüttel

AIRBUS IN HAMBURG 43

The Hamburger Flugzeugbau GmbH factory in 1969, at the time of its merger with Messerschmitt and Bölkow to form MBB. *Hamburger Flugzeugbau GmbH*

A Bv 222 "Wiking" after its completion in Hall 1 of the Finkenwerder factory. *Airbus*

passenger airport with its grass strip had to be chosen, since HFB did not have its own airfield at that time, and the administration, design, and production branches shared Steinwerder Island in Hamburg Harbor with the shipyard. Major components for the Ju 52/3m were built at the shipyard from 1934 onward, with HFB building them on behalf of the State Ministry of Aviation for the Junkers Aircraft Works in Dessau. The military resurgence of the Third Reich not only made HFB economically successful, it also led to the desired know-how in metal-aircraft construction, which the shipbuilders previously employed in production completely lacked. The breakthrough first came, however, with the naming of Dr.-Ing. Richard Vogt as chief designer and technical manager of HFB in 1933. He had previously been employed by Kawasaki in Japan, where under his leadership various metal-aircraft projects had been produced in quantity. At Hamburg he developed eleven aircraft types by 1945, each of which bore his very special signature.

The company's own land-based aircraft and types built under license from other companies were test-flown at Fuhlsbüttel until it was able to open its own company airfield for land aircraft at Wenzendorf, near Buchholz. The seaplanes designed by HFB initially continued to be built in the original factory on Steinwerder and test-flown there, until the uprated production and ever-greater wingspans of the types being built made it necessary for the company to have its own seaplane base. Planning for the new factory began in June 1939 in Hangar 1 of what was then the Finkenwerder Development Works with Land and Water Airports, the current Airbus location.

In 1938, HFB was further integrated into the company and downgraded to a department of the Blohm & Voss shipyard, which was reflected in the designations of aircraft types. The elegant four-engine type 139 mail plane of 1939 still bore the abbreviation "Ha" for Hamburger Flugzeugbau, while the six-engine transatlantic flying boat of 1940, also originally designed for Lufthansa, was designated the Blohm & Voss Bv 222.

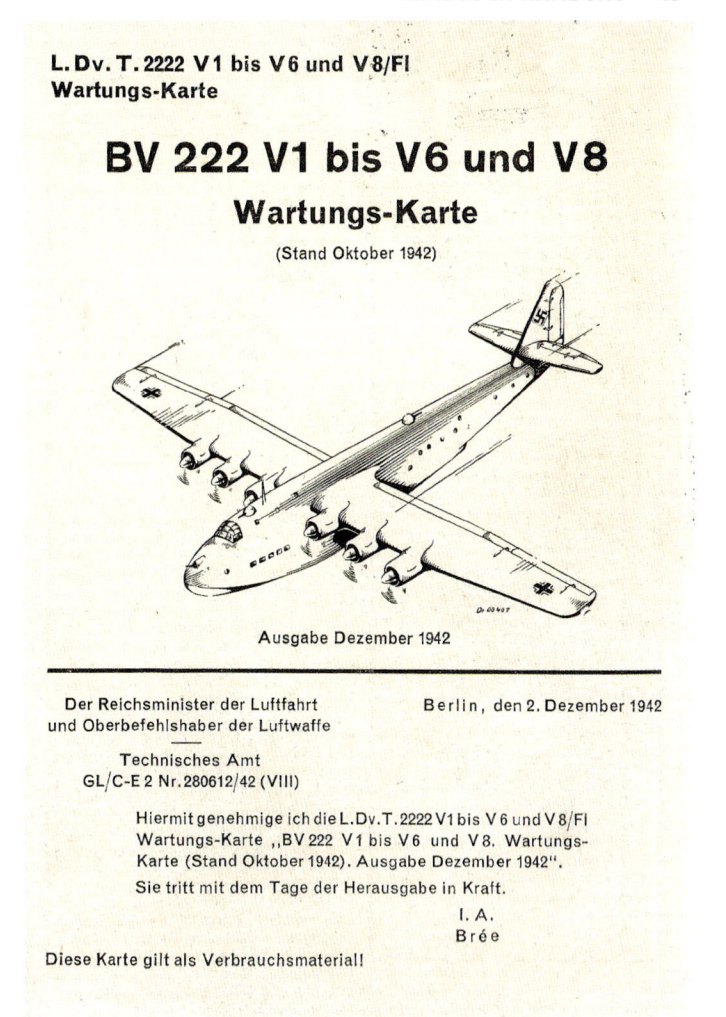

This maintenance card was used by technical personnel as a checklist for the work that had to be carried out on the Bv 222 at various intervals.
Nützel / Borgmann collection

46 AIRBUS A300/310

With the end of the Third Reich, aircraft production by Blohm & Voss also ended in 1945. The factory at Wenzendorf was leveled, and the site was used as a glider airfield and farming operation by the Blohm family, while the Western Allies gave the undamaged factory at Finkenwerder back to the Blohm family in 1955, after the recovery of air sovereignty. With it the family made a new beginning with the Hamburger Flugzeugbau GmbH. Dr. Vogt, who had immigrated to the United States, could not be convinced to return, and his former deputy in the design department, Herman Pohlmann, took over as managing director of the GmbH and as chief designer took over the design and development division. When company patriarch Walter Blohm died in Travemünde on June 13, 1963, his son Werner was already active in the family business. Among his first tasks as head of the HFB construction department was the building in 1955 of the company airfield's runway, which was repeatedly lengthened in the years that followed. Until then, Finkenwerder had been purely a water airport. In 1965, Werner Blohm took over the management of HFB, until 1969, when the company merged with Messerschmitt and Bölkow to become MBB, and until 1974 he remained active as head of the Hamburger Flugzeugbau Division for MBB. He died on March 14, 2018, at the age of ninety-one.

The postwar final-assembly line at Finkenwerder prior to the start of the Airbus program. Nord 2501 Noratlas (1), HFB 320 Hansa Jet and Bölkow Bo 105 helicopter in the foreground (2), plus C-160 Transall (3). *Hamburger Flugzeugbau GmbH*

AIRBUS IN HAMBURG 47

48 AIRBUS A300/310

AIRBUS IN HAMBURG 49

THE TENTATIVE NEW BEGINNING

As in the years 1933 to 1945, the Hamburger Flugzeugbau GmbH, whose company name had never expired and had been reactivated for postwar production, was involved primarily in the production of complete aircraft, such as the Nord 2501 Noratlas and the C-160 Transall, as well as the production of assemblies for the aerospace industry. Its projects included production of the forward fuselage of the Lockheed F-104G Starfighter; the planning, development, and manufacture of the aft fuselage with loading doors for the VTOL Dornier Do 31, fuselage section IV, including engine pods of the Fokker F28 Fellowship; the planning and development of parts of the third stage of the Europa 1 satellite booster rocket; and the final assembly of the Bo 105 helicopter.

In the early years, HFB also began designing its own projects—such as the HFB-209 turboprop airliner. Hermann Pohlmann was directly involved in the design of the CASA C-207 Azor with two piston engines in Spain after the war, and in 1955 he further developed it into the HFB-209. The project failed, however, due to the negative response from Lufthansa, its potential first customer, which preferred a proven type from foreign production such as the Vickers Viscount.

The HFB-314 jet airliner, first presented in 1957 and designed to carry up to seventy passengers in a comfortable 2 + 2 seating arrangement, also failed. Its maximum takeoff weight was supposed to be 88,736 pounds. HFB was fully aware that a completely independent development would overextend the small company financially and in terms of personnel, and it therefore sought partners at home and abroad. While other West German manufacturers—such as Heinkel—were working on comparable designs and were therefore not interested in cooperation, the HFB team also failed to interest Sud Aviation in France or the Dutch Fokker company in joint pan-European production. In a conversation with the author, Professor Ernst Simon, then active as head of the technical selection committee for new Lufthansa types, explained the HFB 314 drama from Lufthansa's point of view:

Cover of a C-160 sales brochure. *Hamburger Flugzeugbau GmbH*

With the German economic miracle the German aviation industry also became active again. In order to again make it competitive in the civil field, in 1957 the Ministry of Economics under Ludwig Erhardt organized a competition for German airliner designs. HFB entered the competition with its HFB 314, a fast twin-jet, medium-range aircraft for seventy passengers, whose concept was undoubtedly very promising and could certainly have kept pace with the competing Caravelle. Heinkel also presented two versions of a small, fast, short-range aircraft—the propeller-driven He 211A and the twin-jet He 211B. The two were also remarkable designs. We dealt intensively with these designs and discussed the many technical questions with their designers, Hans Wocke at HFB and Siegfried Günter at Heinkel—both once famous names. Finally, in 1958, Lufthansa gave its recommendation to the Federal Ministry of Economics to further promote the HFB 314 and He 211B with government funds, at least until the solidly verifiable design phase had been completed.

What many had feared happened—the federal German finance minister Franz Etzel (CDU) balked, and in 1960, both companies were forced to stop work due to lack of funding.

Like Hermann Pohlmann, HFB 314 project leader Dipl.-Ing. Hans Wocke had his professional roots at Junkers in Dessau. As head of development he had been closely involved with the design of the world's first multiengine jet bomber, the Ju 287. Its most noteworthy feature: the Ju 287 had forward-swept wings. It was a significant design feature that would again gain importance in the early 1960s. After the war ended, Wocke, like many other Junkers engineers in Dachau, was moved with his family to Podberesye, near Moscow, where he continued development of the Ju 287, which became the EF 131, also with negatively swept wings. Not until 1954 was Wocke allowed to return to the German Democratic Republic, founded in 1949, where he initially found a new professional home at the Union of State-Owned Enterprises (VVB) Aircraft Works in Dresden. Four years later Wocke went looking for a new challenge in Hamburg, West Germany, which took place before the wall was erected along the border between the two Germanys—yet, a return to the DDR was out of the question for him.

His flight was successful, and Hans Wocke would go on to develop his masterpiece, the HFB 320 Hansa Jet, as head of the design bureau and deputy chief designer at Hamburger Flugzeugbau.

Takeoff preparations by the second Hansa Jet prototype, with the registration D-CLOU, which in the summer of 2018 could be seen in the Deutsches Museum in Munich. Designed and built in Finkenwerder, the HFB 320 was the first jet airliner produced in Germany. *Hamburger Flugzeugbau GmbH*

THE FORWARD-SWEPT WING

When the Hamburger Flugzeugbau GmbH (HFB) unveiled its HFB 320 project at the beginning of the 1960s, Hawker-Siddeley, Dassault, Lockheed, Grumman, North American, and Lear dominated the market for business jets. In June 1963, HFB presented its HFB 320 to an international professional audience for the first time at the Aerosalon at Paris Le Bourget. In addition to various sales brochures, the Hamburg company had brought with it to Paris a mockup of the aircraft's fuselage, which clearly showed the size difference between the Hansa Jet and the other business jet types.

The aircraft's midmounted wings had 15 degrees of forward sweep, and their linking structure passed through the fuselage aft of the passenger cabin. This made it possible for the Hamburger Flugzeugbau to conceive a "wide-body" jet with unique cabin dimensions for its category. Thus the continuous standing height was 5.74 feet, the maximum fuselage width was 6.2 feet, and the passenger cabin was a full 15 feet long.

Because of its certification as a full-fledged airliner, the Hansa Jet was used in scheduled commuter services by various American and Canadian airlines. This airline version of the aircraft accommodated two pilots, twelve passengers, and a stewardess. In addition to a spacious onboard toilet, the HFB 320 had a small pantry for onboard meals.

Production of the Hansa Jet involved international cooperation and was thus a small foretaste of the later Airbus program. The aft fuselage and tail section were made by CASA in Spain, the undercarriage came from Lockheed's British subsidiary, the wings were made by SIAT in Donauwörth, the General Electric engines came from the United States, the fuselage came from HFB's plant in Stade, and the final assembly into a complete aircraft took place at HFB in Hamburg-Finkenwerder.

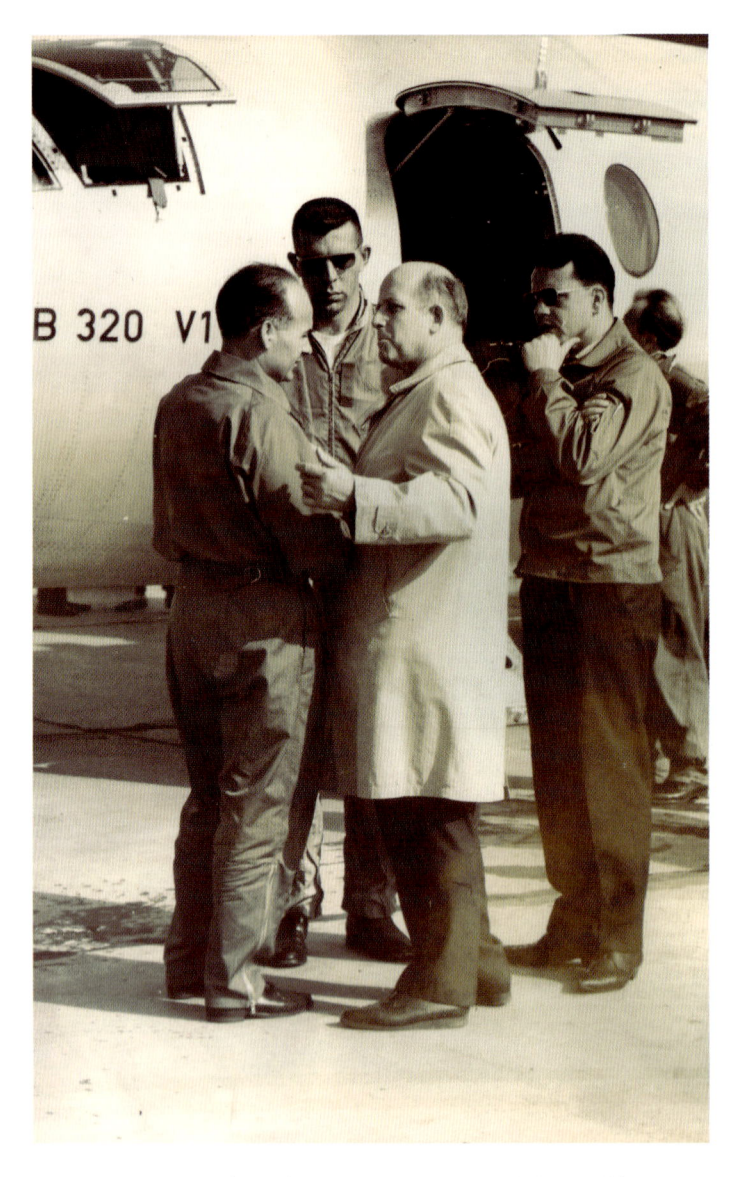

Dipl.-Ing. Hans Wocke (center), who went on to become chairman of the managing board and Airbus A300 program director in 1967, in conversation with Hansa Jet test pilots Bardill, Davis, and Bartels (from left to right). The photo was taken the day the HFB 320 V1, registered D-CHFB, made its maiden flight, April 21, 1964. Hamburger Flugzeugbau GmbH

The HFB 320 V1 prototype with the registration D-CHFB took off from Hamburg on its seventy-three-minute maiden flight on April 21, 1964. With chief test pilot Loren William "Swede" Davis at the controls, the aircraft lifted off at 10:29, and after the flight controls, trim, flaps, and air brakes had been tested, it landed at Lemwerder, near Bremen. After the first flight of the Hansa Jet, Davis said: "This aircraft with its forward-swept wing demonstrated good flight characteristics during this first test. I have flown many types of aircraft and am convinced that this new structural shape will meet all expectations." After a three-year test phase, on February 21, 1967, the Hansa Jet received its German type certification, followed a few weeks later by its American certification.

The HFB 320's unusual design, to which Loren Davis referred in his comments on the first flight, offered various advantages. In addition to improved low-speed flight characteristics, the passengers had an unhindered view of the world beneath them, unobstructed by the wing. An even bigger positive, however, was the spacious cabin, which was not crossed by a wing spar as in most competing designs. HFB exploited this opportunity in an optimal fashion and conceived the Hansa Jet with a quick-change configuration. Thus, in addition to an airliner with twelve seats, the buyer of an HFB 320 also had a freighter or seven-seat VIP aircraft. Conversion from one version to another took from ten to a maximum of thirty-five minutes. As if this was not enough, HFB also developed a training version for training would-be pilots, which was ordered by the Dutch national aviation school at Eelde. Most eye-catching, however, was the HBF 320 ECM version for the Luftwaffe with its various antennas, which was used as an electronic-warfare trainer.

A total of forty-seven Hansa Jets were built: two prototypes and forty-five production aircraft. The HFB 330 Fan Jet, a developed version with an extended fuselage and quieter and more fuel-efficient Garrett ATF-3 turbofan engines, was presented to the public in 1969; however, it was never built. Messerschmitt-Bölkow-Blohm (MBB), with which the Hamburger Flugzeugbau merged that same year, saw itself forced to divert all civil investment into the beginning Airbus project.

The former main administration of the Hamburger Flugzeugbau GmbH became the seat of the Hamburg Division of MBB after the merger with Messerschmitt and Bölkow. *MBB*

Of the forty-seven aircraft built, none remain flyable; however, the members of the nonprofit association "Ein HANSA JET für Hamburg e.V." are working in their free time to return a HFB 320 to airworthy condition. The fifth production aircraft made its first flight in December 1969 and is to be licensed in Germany as a unique historical specimen. The association is a guest of Airbus at Finkenwerder and, in the future, plans to display its Hansa Jet at home and abroad as a flying ambassador for Hamburg as an aviation location.

IN SEARCH OF PARTNERS

As important as the Hansa Jet project was from a local political point of view, it failed to pay off economically for HFB. This was true despite the personal commitment of Werner Blohm, who personally carried out sales negotiations with potential customers and, whenever possible, accompanied interested parties on demonstration flights in the Hansa Jet. In the end there was no getting around taking the path desired by the federal government toward the concentration of the German aviation industry and searching for business partners. On August 31, 1967, the HFB management level held initial talks with the chairman of the supervisory board of the Vereinigte Flugtechnische Werke (VFW), based in Bremen. HFB management then noted that "The future financial freedom of movement of the Hamburger Flugzeugbau depends largely on the further development of sales of the HFB 320 Hansa. HFB is linked to the HFB 320 Hansa in such a way that achieving success with it is a fateful question." There followed a year of discussions about a good path into the future among Hamburger Flugzeugbau, rivals, government authorities, and the City of Hamburg—and this against the background of further stagnating sales of the Hansa Jet. How precarious the situation was in early 1968 is shown by the fact that HFB had to use all of its available lines of credit for months, and despite this it just managed to pay the wages and salaries of its employees at the end of the month. Rescue came with the sale of three HFB 320s to the Dutch national aviation school in Eelde, whose proceeds again put some funds into the empty coffers.

By the end of June 1969, the Hansa Jet program had cost 139 million marks. HFB itself had borne 87.2 million of this, while the federal government granted 40.7 million marks as a success loan. As well, thanks to its guarantee, the free and Hanseatic city of Hamburg granted a credit of more than 11.1 million marks. HFB could afford the high-deficit Hansa Jet program thanks only to profits from the Noratlas, Transall, and Starfighter projects—but even that was not enough. After HFB asked the federal government for another surety of fifty million marks, the government lost its patience and demanded the merger with one of the company's competitors it had requested a year earlier.

At the end of 1968, the German aviation industry consisted of the large companies Bölkow, Dornier, Hamburger Flugzeugbau, Heinkel, Messerschmitt, and Vereinigte Flugtechnische Werke, whose owners were ordered to the Ministry of Economics on December 4 of that year. After announcing funding programs by the federal government for the Airbus and MRCA Tornado programs, the representatives of the companies were asked about their readiness to merge. When Werner Blohm's turn came, he categorically declared himself ready for a merger. The Hamburger Flugzeugbau was officially on the lookout for a bride.

LOSS OF INDEPENDENCE

After the sale of a single Hansa Jet to the German Research Institute for Air and Space Travel, based in Brunswick, HFB began 1969—which was to be its last year as an independent company—with a small financial cushion. The takeover merry-go-round began to go round with VFW in Bremen and Fokker of the Netherlands, which wanted to add HFB as a third member of the team. At the same time, Messerschmitt-Bölkow offered a merger with HFB. In the course of the negotiations, Werner Blohm was mistakenly handed the annual plan of the two southern German merger partners, in which at first glance he noticed a major problem: neither Messerschmitt nor Bölkow could meet their obligations with respect to engineering services and work packages resulting from their participation in the Airbus program. Armed with this knowledge, in the course of negotiations Blohm succeeded in bringing the entire Airbus program to Hamburg. Thanks to the HFB 320 Hansa Jet, the city was the

AIRBUS IN HAMBURG   55

For the HFB 320, which was built in a pan-European cooperative effort, the Hamburger Flugzeugbau GmbH developed a global spare-parts supply system for its customers that operated twenty-four hours a day, seven days a week, 365 days a year. Shown here is a cutaway drawing of the HFB 320 freight version. A Hansa Jet could be converted from a seven-seat VIP jet into a commuter jet carrying twelve passengers in thirty minutes, and in another thirty minutes it could be turned into a freighter. *Hamburger Flugzeugbau GmbH*

only location in Germany specialized in the building of civil aircraft. When the merger contract was signed on June 11, 1969, HFB's independence as a company ended, for which the Blohm family was compensated with 35.5 percent of the shares in the new MBB.

Werner Blohm stayed on as manager of MBB's Hamburger Flugzeugbau Division (UH) until November 1, 1974, when, after losses and accusations of poor management, he resigned under pressure from the co-owners. Ludwig Bölkow, in particular, was a driving force behind the commercially motivated sacking of Werner Blohm. After the founding family no longer had any influence over the corporate business, they collectively decided to sell their remaining shares in the company. Hamburg and Bavaria vied for the Blohm shares in what resembled a north-south crime novel. The family had already promised these to the Bavarians when the Bavarian Landesbank that was handling the negotiations requested renegotiation, and the Blohms thus felt themselves no longer bound by their promise.

This was Hamburg's hour. Its mayor, Ulrich Klose, saw his chance and immediately had a contractual text drawn up to acquire the Blohm family's 20 percent blocking stake in MBB. On June 1, 1976, Hamburg not only bought the mentioned shares from the fourteen shareholders of the Blohm family for sixty-six million deutsch marks but, by purchasing them, also acquired the related say on location decisions and thus secured the future of Airbus production in Hamburg.

The Hamburg-Finkenwerder Airbus factory in 2018. This photo was taken from the same perspective as the one on page 43, taken in 1969. *Airbus Operations GmbH*

CHAPTER 5
THE A300 STORY
FROM POLITICAL ISSUE TO AIRLINER

A PESSIMIST SEES THE DIFFICULTY IN EVERY OPPORTUNITY; AN OPTIMIST SEES THE OPPORTUNITY IN EVERY DIFFICULTY. —Winston Churchill, British prime minister (1940–45 and 1951–55)

After the first studies by the future Airbus partners in 1965 and 1966, in the summer of 1967 a design crystallized from them, which in its approach was very reminiscent of the A300B that was later produced. The key data of this concept, already called the A300, as of June 30 of that year were the following:

- **Wingspan:** 148 feet
- **Length:** 160 feet
- **Fuselage diameter:** 21 feet
- **Passenger capacity:** maximum of 298
- **Maximum range:** 1,926 miles
- **Cruise speed:** 574 mph

The Airbus planners considered themselves to be on the right track with their design, primarily on the basis of market research and personal conversations with the leading airlines in Europe and the United States. The Airbus was supposed to help the airlines handle the rapidly growing scheduled freight and tourist traffic in the short- and medium-range sectors. In the United States alone, traffic volume in the Airbus market segment grew by 12 percent between 1964 and 1967. In the mid-1960s, the booming tourist traffic in Europe grew by 30 percent, and even air freight promised the Airbus market researchers a rosy future on European routes.

These positive signals caused the Airbus team to assume that even if market development leveled off, several hundred A300s would be needed by 1985 just to handle the growth in traffic. They estimated the worldwide requirement for aircraft with an operating range of less than 2,237 miles for the year 1989 to be 1,500 machines. On the basis of these advance calculations, they calculated that European Airbus traffic amounting to a volume of 6,000 and more passengers daily on a series of scheduled service routes could be expected, while it was estimated that other routes, primarily tourist, would carry passenger traffic of about 3,000 passengers per day. The key conclusion by the Airbus managers: with the existing small

LEFT The Airbus triumvirate of the 1960s (*from left to right*): Dr. Bernhard Weinhardt (chairman of Deutsche Airbus GmbH), Henri Ziegler (president of Airbus Industrie), and Franz Josef Strauß (Airbus Industrie chairman of the board). Without their tenacity, the project for a pan-European wide-body jet would have made a belly landing long before its first flight. *Deutsche Airbus GmbH*

OPPOSITE Cutaway drawing of the originally planned A300, with a fuselage diameter of 21 feet and 3 + 3 + 3 seating. This version was completely oversized for the European and American air traffic markets. *Hamburger Flugzeugbau GmbH*

passenger jets with 100 to 150 seats, such as the BAC 111, Boeing 727, or Hawker-Siddeley Trident, European and American airports would quickly reach the limits of their capacity in the terminals and on the runways. The answer could only be a large jet in the style of the A300.

It was obvious to the Airbus designers that their A300 would have to be an airliner incorporating the latest technology in all areas of aircraft construction, whether it was the materials used, equipment, navigation equipment, or the requirements for bad-weather landings. These premises were formulated in the following expectations of their own design:

- low transport costs (30% lower than contemporaneous medium-range jets)
- short ground times
- low maintenance costs
- long service life
- high degree of flight safety
- usability on tourist routes
- transport of air freight in containers and on pallets
- possibility of further development

The Airbus planners gave priority to designing an aircraft built for economy rather than one with a high cruising speed. They instead sought to achieve short travel times by optimally designing the passenger cabin. This was a special issue for the German Airbus group and a thematic remnant of the "Airbus system," which had also included fast train connections at the airports and newly-designed air-rail terminals with extremely short transfer times between aircraft and train. After these futuristic ideas had to give way to financial reality, the Airbus team concentrated on the aircraft and its optimal layout. To reduce turnaround times on the ground, a rapid flow of passengers during boarding and disembarking was a focal point for the engineers. Special attention was paid to the arrangement of the two aisles in the cabin and the number and size of the doors, as well as corresponding ground installations for passenger handling. Another criterion was the existing requirement for all passengers to be evacuated within ninety seconds in an emergency—in 1967, this was only a "recommendation" by the American FAA. The fuselage cross section of 21 feet enabled a plan with nine seats per row (3 + 3 + 3), which were divided by two aisles. The passenger cabin was not divided in the one-class concept, so that in contemporaneous drawings it resembles a large cinema auditorium. The A300 was to have six doors—two each in the front and rear for entrance and exit, and two large emergency exits over the wings. The washrooms were envisaged in the tail of the aircraft, while the kitchens were arranged in front of and behind the passenger cabin.

After the planning group had reviewed the operational statistics of European and North American air traffic, it came to the conclusion that the Airbus should be operated not only from large airports, but from smaller regional airports as well. In 1967, the aircraft's takeoff distance at maximum gross weight was set at 6,660 feet, while landing distance at maximum landing weight was supposed to be just 5,413 feet. In the 1960s. the Airbus team around Henri Ziegler, Roger Béteille, Felix Kracht, and chairman of the board Franz Josef Strauß found itself facing allegations that the twin-engined A300 was not safe. Three engines, such as on the McDonnell Douglas DC-10 or Lockheed L-1011, was the benchmark for a wide-body aircraft. Airbus responded to this criticism by pointing out the high dependability of the jet engines then in use in passenger aircraft. The RB 207-03 three-shaft turbofan planned for use in the A300 was supposed to develop 47,434 pounds of thrust for takeoff, with a bypass ratio of 1:5. This meant that the engine's forward fan directed five times as much air around the turbofan engine as through the core of the engine.

An experimental engine with the designation RB 178-16, a twin-shaft design with the same high-pressure section and that thermodynamically and in terms of size was identical to the planned RB 207, was already running on the Rolls-Royce test stand in 1967.

Airbus justified mounting the engines beneath the wings with the advantages of easier access for maintenance personnel and lower structural weight compared to placing them in the tail. All of this was true to the initial strategy: look for solutions that avoid design complications and in later operation make possible short turnaround times on the ground.

THE A300 LOSES WEIGHT

The first concrete A300 variants of the summer of 1967 lasted just a few months. That September the rather chubby-looking A300 shrank to become the A300B, with a fuselage diameter of 18.5 feet and a cabin width of 17.7 feet. The subsequent A300B2/B4, A300-600, A310, A340, and even (in summer 2018) the A330 all were produced with this standard measurement unchanged. The length of the planned wide-body jet varied repeatedly until April 1969, when Airbus committed itself to the ultimate 176 feet for the production version. The reduction in fuselage cross section and other design alterations resulted in the A300B's empty weight being 27.55 tons less than that of the original A300 design.

When in April 1969 Rolls-Royce announced that it was replacing the RB 207 program with the RB 211, with which the British engine maker calculated that it would have good sales prospects, especially as a part of American projects, the Airbus development team was initially in shock. The A300B had lost is only envisaged power plant.

But as technical director of the Airbus project, Roger Béteille was first to recognize the opportunities this offered. This withdrawal provided the opportunity to design the Airbus A300B so that it could accept all the large turbofan engines of the day, such as the General Electric CF6-50, Pratt & Whitney JT9D, and Rolls-Royce RB 211. Out of solidarity with Rolls-Royce, in 1969 Airbus initially specified the RB 211 as the only standard engine, but by the spring of 1970 the airlines could also select the General Electric CF6-50 as an alternative, and soon after it became the standard engine of the A300B. Only

Airbus originally offered installation of the kitchen on the lower deck, analogous to the Lockheed L-1011. This solution was not, however, very practical for short flights, since serving the meals and drinks, which were delivered by elevator to the passenger cabin, would have taken much too much time. And so in the early 1970s this idea disappeared back into the design bureau's filing cabinets. *Airbus International, Paris*

Iberia and SAS chose the Pratt & Whitney JT9D, which was offered as an alternative. The RB 211, which was theoretically available again from 1972 onward, was not chosen by a single airline. How foresighted the decision by Airbus was to immediately switch to several families of engines was shown in 1971 by the disaster of the Lockheed L-1011 TriStar. Its developer had selected the RB 211 as the sole engine type, and its unavailability after Rolls-Royce's temporary insolvency initially contributed to considerable delays—and finally to the economic failure of the L-1011 program. One of the customers lost through the Rolls-Royce insolvency was Lufthansa, which had already decided in favor of the Lockheed L-1011 and against the competing McDonnell Douglas DC-10-30. Because the long-range version of the TriStar could no longer be offered when the purchase decision was made, Lufthansa was forced to select the DC-10.

COMFORT JET

Not only the most effective but also the most comfortable possible transport of passengers was the focus of the Airbus design team. This included the cabin layout with eight seats per row, so that no passenger sat more than one place from the aisle, and the unpopular middle seat was largely eliminated. Leaving nothing to chance, in 1969 SNIAS in Toulouse and Deutsche Airbus in Munich-Allach each built a complete mockup for development of an optimized Airbus cabin. Meanwhile, another mockup, which Airbus later used for sales negotiations at the Aérosalon at Paris Le Bourget, took shape in the HFB factory in Hamburg-Finkenwerder. Lockable luggage compartments above the seats were also standard features of the A300B cabin, and onboard kitchens beneath the floor were offered as an option, from which meals would be moved by elevators to the passenger cabin. This was a feature that Lockheed offered as standard in its L-1011 wide-body jet, but it was not, however, selected by any Airbus A300 customer. Airbus passengers had to forgo one comfort feature of other jets: the A300B had no individual fresh-air nozzles above the seats—it did, however, have an effective air-conditioning system, which not only made possible temperatures between 15 and 30 degrees Celsius (59 to 86 degrees F) but also provided a constant exchange of air and a comfortable cabin pressure height of 5,900 feet at a flying altitude of 34,777 feet.

In 1970 the time had finally come. After five years of planning, drawing, rejecting, and drawing again, the first parts were completed in the factories of the European Airbus partners. About fifteen months after the official program launch on May 29, 1969, according to plan, 20 percent of the envisaged costs up to type certification had been spent. For the factory in Hamburg, August 4, 1971, was a big day. Accompanied by a press event, in which the chairman of the Deutsche Airbus GmbH, Dr. Bernhard Weinhardt, and Felix Kracht, technical director of Airbus Industrie, took part, the first aft fuselage for the A300B1 prototype was completed by the Hamburger Flugzeugbau Division of the Messerschmitt-Bölkow-Blohm GmbH and released for transport to France for final assembly. This was not the first assembly delivered from Finkenwerder to Toulouse, a so-called section 15 having made the journey on March 8 of that year. But with a length of almost 65 feet, including transport device, and a weight of 8.8 tons, the aft fuselage, which was delivered in August, was the first German major component and thus of special importance.

Its transport initially took place by ship from the factory dock in Finkenwerder via the Elbe, the North Sea, and the North Atlantic to the French port city of Bordeaux. From there the trip continued overland by special trailer to Toulouse for final assembly. The Airbus Super Guppy transport aircraft was not used for this task because the first example of the flying special transport did not become operational until mid-September 1971. To avoid delays in completion of the A300B1 and avoid threatening the deadline for the first flight, Airbus chose to transport all the components for the first prototype by land and sea. In some cases this led to stressful situations as the heavy transports made their way through the narrow streets of southern French villages, which they could negotiate only with great care. Incidentally, this mode of transport was rediscovered by Airbus on account of the huge dimensions of the A380 components for production of its megaliner, and it has been practiced successfully since 2004—albeit over improved roads.

The assembly for the first A300B1 that went on the road in 1971 consisted of the entire section of the roughly 164-foot-long wide-body fuselage aft of the wing. Production of individual parts for the aft fuselage began in Hamburg in April 1970, and the production process until the assembly's arrival in Toulouse took all of seventeen months. In the course of quantity production, the company was able to reduce the assembly time for the A300B2/B4 to about ten months. Safety and reliability of the structure and systems, as well as low production costs, were guiding principles for the Airbus consortium even as the A300B1 was being built. To keep production costs low and shorten the cycle time, it used the latest production methods, such as metal bonding and chemical removal. High-stress A300B components were also designed as modules. The managers of MBB's Hamburg Division were especially proud of their acquisition of a stretch-forming press with a pulling force of 275.6 tons and a stamping force of 441 tons, with which skinning and reinforcing plates for Airbus production could be formed precisely to the millimeter.

On March 8, 1971, the first Airbus fuselage section 15 completed in Hamburg (*1*) was shipped from Hamburg to St. Nazaire by the coastal freighter *Eduard Kähler* (*2*). This faded photo shows that the section was packed in a wooden crate, and here it is seen on the hook of the crane originally created in the 1940s to lift Blohm & Voss seaplanes. Section 15 comprises the upper fuselage above the wing center section, which in France was completed with the wing center-section box and lower fuselage. *MBB*

Components for the second prototype arrived in Toulouse not just from Hamburg, but from all over Europe, in the only Super Guppy transport then in use. These included fuselage sections 13 and 14, made by VFW in Einswarden, at the mouth of the Weser. They were first taken by ship to nearby Lemwerder and then loaded into the Airbus transport aircraft for delivery to France for final assembly. There were the wings, which were equipped by VFW-Fokker in Bremen, which also reached their final destination by Super Guppy. September 26, 1972, was a big day for Airbus. At the official rollout, the corporation was finally able to present to the assembled employees, the press, potential customers, and, not least, the politicians of the partner nations not just drawings and models but a real aircraft they could touch: the first of two A300B1 prototypes. But it was not until the maiden flight on October 28 that the dream of a European wide-body airliner finally became a reality. Onboard this flight, which wrote aviation history, was Airbus chief test pilot Max Fischl as captain, copilot Bernard Ziegler, and flight test engineers Pierre Canell, Romeo Zinzoni, and Günter Scherer. After an extensive test program involving four aircraft—the two B1 prototypes and two B2 production aircraft—on March 15, 1974, the A300B became the first aircraft to simultaneously receive its German and French type certifications. The American FAA followed with its recognition two months later.

Cover of an Airbus Industrie sales prospectus from April 1970. *Airbus Industrie*

The A300B2 with the registration D-AIAA was the first Airbus delivered to Lufthansa. The aircraft's modern lines are noteworthy even today. *Lufthansa*

LUFTHANSA AND THE A300

While France for reasons of policy ordered six A300B2s on November 3, 1971, Deutsche Lufthansa needed persuading to follow suit. Although like Air France it was 100 percent state owned, the German airline's senior management always placed great importance on an independent selection of aircraft types in the best interests of the airline. The German government was forced to discover this in 1965, when Lufthansa vehemently withstood political pressure and selected the American Boeing 737 instead of the British BAC 111. The Lufthansa managers preferred risking a political altercation on the European stage rather than be bullied by politicians in their selection of aircraft. History now repeated itself five years later, when German politicians pressed Lufthansa to purchase the A300 and caused the public to wonder about the unyielding attitude of its national carrier.

On September 6, 1967, Gerhard Höltje—who as the airline's board member in charge of engineering was responsible for the selection of its aircraft types—formulated Lufthansa's fundamental thinking on the question of the European Airbus. In this paper, Höltje wrote: "Lufthansa had, however, like the majority of other European airlines, made it clear from the beginning that in its situation the use of such aircraft was unlikely to become necessary before 1975." The justification provided by Höltje was the order for Boeing 727s, and in particular its stretched 200 version with a seating capacity of about 160, which was capable of meeting Lufthansa's traffic requirements until the mid-1970s. To nip any doubts in the bud and lend emphasis to his words, Höltje added: "Lufthansa reserves to itself full freedom of decision in the selection of the most-favorable aircraft for its special circumstances, meaning that if an aircraft becomes necessary only for the 1975 summer traffic, the awarding of the contract does not need to take place prior to the first half of 1973!" In order to have an optimal selection opportunity, Höltje expected of Airbus that it would offer Lufthansa various aircraft at the appropriate time, "from which, using the selection system developed by it, it can select the most suitable machine for Lufthansa's purposes." For this reason, Lufthansa was unable to give a binding opinion or assessment of the Airbus program after completion of the Airbus definition phase, expected in 1968. Höltje: "In this case it would, violating all the laws of economical thinking, sacrifice the possibilities that lay in developments in the years from 1969 until the beginning of 1973." In fact, Lufthansa would not become an Airbus customer in 1973, not placing its order for three A300B2s until June 25, 1975, for delivery beginning in February 1976.

Three-man cockpit of a Lufthansa A300B2. *Lufthansa*

The situation was different in the area of technical cooperation with the Airbus team. Since the early days of the postwar Lufthansa, established in 1953, its technical management cultivated a close technical-experience exchange with manufacturers of commercial aircraft around the globe—including the Airbus developers. This constructive collaboration was, as Gerhard Höltje formulated it in his fundamental thinking, "very lively" between the individual designers of the Airbus consortium and Lufthansa. Lufthansa engineers advised the employees of the Airbus partner companies on, among other things, the functional construction of individual assemblies and systems and offered the ability to study them in detail in other aircraft types in the Lufthansa workshops during layovers.

Lufthansa was also—like Air France and British European Airways (BEA)—on the Airline Steering Committee and participated in eleven specialist teams, which together with the manufacturer were supposed to determine the final design of the A300B by the end of April 1968, in just two months. Höltje stated on behalf of Lufthansa that he thought that creating a complete specification coordinated with the airlines in such a short time was impossible. In fact the various proposals by the airlines were not included in the A300 design specification of April 30, 1968. As described in an earlier chapter, the A300 was originally a politically desired project to promote European unification. And so the participating ministers from France, Germany, and Great Britain decided by way of a Ministries Outline Specification what the new wide-body airliner would look like. The original concept included neither the proposals made at the meeting of airlines in London on October 22, 1965, nor those made in Paris on June 13, 1966. The result was an aircraft not attuned to prevailing market conditions, and it was unanimously rejected by the airlines. The completely inadequate, in Höltje's view, cabin and systems equipment of the A300 as offered by Airbus gave cause for criticism. To raise the A300's standard equipment at least to the level usual in aircraft construction worldwide, Airbus at first demanded considerable surcharges from the potential buyers. Not just Höltje as Lufthansa's representative but also BEA chairman Sir Anthony Milward complained publicly about the inadequacies of the Airbus. This was reason enough for its manufacturer consortium to go back into detail planning and postpone the ultimate design freeze until 1969—and thus in the end produce an aircraft in line with market requirements.

THE LUFTHANSA REQUIREMENTS

In 1968, Lufthansa formulated requirements for a short- and medium-range aircraft with a high seating capacity and submitted them to Airbus:

- the aircraft to be supplied with a type certification corresponding to FAR 25
- seating, pure economy version: 250 seats ± 10 percent
- cargo-hold volume in relation to passenger seating: 8.8 cubic feet per seat
- maximum payload: 75,265 pounds
- cruise speed comparable to that of the Boeing 727
- maximum range achievable with 50 percent payload
- maximum takeoff runway length at 89.6°F, max. takeoff weight, 0 wind: 8,497 feet
- maximum landing-runway length at sea level: 5,577 feet
- approach speed: maximum 125 knots at maximum landing weight
- range with 61,729 pounds payload: 1,243 miles
- seat kilometer costs at least 15 percent lower than those of the Boeing 727-200 with 155 seats
- structural durability of 40,000 flying hours without major repairs to the airframe
- departure punctuality of 99 percent (with five-minute waiting period)

The Italian airline Alitalia was also a member of the ATLAS consortium when it worked out its A300B definition in 1971. It was not until seven years later that the airline ordered A300B4s. *Borgmann collection*

THE ATLAS GROUP

In addition to these direct discussions with the manufacturer, Lufthansa primarily worked on the specification for the A300B within the ATLAS Group, formed in 1968 for its partner airlines Air France, Alitalia, Lufthansa, and Sabena, which were joined by the Spanish airline Iberia in 1972. Like the comparable KSSU group of KLM, Swissair, SAS, and UTA, ATLAS was also founded for definition of technical standards and the allocation of maintenance and repair tasks for the relatively small partial fleets of its partners. In the ATLAS consortium, for example, from 1969 onward Air France took responsibility for the major overhaul (D check) of the small number of Boeing 747s operated by its partners. Lufthansa was selected as the overhaul center for 747 engines, and Alitalia and Sabena took over responsibility for overhauling 747 components. Another agreement concerned a 747 flight simulator, which Lufthansa also operated for the ATLAS airlines. A subcommittee also concerned itself with the study of new aircraft projects and the development of common technical standards for these new jets. At the beginning of 1971, ATLAS consortium determined that the next wide-body jets for its members would probably be the McDonnell Douglas DC-10 and the Airbus A300, and on behalf of the partner airlines, it immediately engaged their manufacturers in an intensive definition process.

The ATLAS partners wasted no time and at the end of January arranged their first working meeting with Airbus representatives. Eight bilateral ATLAS-Airbus teams were formed, which on a technical level dealt with the subject areas of performance, operating economy, flight noise, definition of the cockpit, the electronic systems, the aircraft structure, the cabin layout, the engine selection, the layout of hydraulics and flight controls, and cabin air-conditioning. A ninth team was given authority to conclude concrete contracts with Airbus on the basis of the stipulations made by teams 1 to 8.

In addition to the Airbus basic layout of the A300, by July 1971 the ATLAS technicians came up with more than 1,000 requests for changes. Most of them were marginal demands, some of which involved only formulations in the technical documents, yet 300 more-significant master changes remained, whose implementation was negotiated between Airbus management and the ATLAS committee. On October 7, 1971, the ATLAS representatives presented their findings concerning the anticipated profitability of the A300B on the route networks of the four partners. As well, they had designed standard sales contracts for Air France, Alitalia, Lufthansa, and Sabena concerning the A300B on the basis of the ATLAS specification for the aircraft type. Not ATLAS but rather the individual airlines subsequently ordered their aircraft in direct negotiations with Airbus. They were authorized to deviate from ATLAS standards in details, provided the fundamental idea of a common layout of the A300 was not torn to pieces as a result. The agreement applied both to the A300B2 and, from a technical viewpoint, the identical B4 variant with a higher gross weight. As in the case of the Boeing 747, the cooperative partners shared the maintenance tasks for their Airbus aircraft among themselves, with Lufthansa responsible for major overhauls (D checks) of the partner aircraft at its workshops in Hamburg, and Air France for the engines.

Altogether, Lufthansa invested about 5,000 engineering hours in the A300 project phase and expended another 20,000 hours in working on the aircraft specification. This involvement led to about 1,500 changes in the basic layout of the A300 and thus to significant technical and economic improvements to the aircraft. In cooperation with Airbus Industrie and the authorities, Lufthansa Technik further developed the maintenance system for the A300B, which added another 6,000 hours of work. Lufthansa thus indisputably had a major share in the A300's success.

THE A300 STORY   69

Sabena of Belgium did not order the A300B; instead, in the 1980s and 1990s, it maintained a fleet of up to six A310s. *Sabena*

Impressions of the interior of a Lufthansa A300-600 in the 1990s. First-class service (1) and the rear economy-class cabin (2). *Lufthansa*

Pope John Paul II entrusted himself to Lufthansa and its A300B during his visit to Germany in November 1980 (3). *Lufthansa*

CHAPTER 6
ALLOCATION OF A300B WORK SHARES IN SEPTEMBER 1970

IN THE ENTIRE PROJECT

VFW-Fokker (based in Dusseldorf)	11%
Dornier	4%
MBB	21%
SNIAS	43%
Hawker-Siddeley	17%
Fokker-VFW (based in Amsterdam)	4%

WITHIN GERMANY

VFW-Fokker (based in Dusseldorf)	30%
Dornier	10%
MBB	60%

CONSTRUCTION BREAKDOWN

SNIAS: cockpit and section 12
VFW-Fokker: section 13
SNIAS: center-section–wing root transition, section 21
MBB: upper shell, section 15; entire fuselage end, sections 16 to 19, with vertical stabilizer and rudder
MBB / VFW-Fokker (each 50%): horizontal stabilizer
Hawker-Siddeley Aviation: wing center section
Fokker-VFW: movable wing parts
General Electric: engines
McDonnell Douglas: engine pods
MBB and VFW: engine pylons
Messier: undercarriage

Hapag Lloyd Flug used the A300B4 on its network of routes to southern European vacation destinations. *Hapag-Lloyd / TUIfly*

An A300B4 of Malaysia Airline System (MAS) is towed into a hangar of the Hamburg factory for fitting out of the cabin. MAS initially ordered three examples of this type on August 30, 1978, contributing to the then badly needed upswing in Airbus's fortunes. *MBB*

Thai Airways advertisement for its flight program in the winter of 1978–79. *Borgmann collection*

GERMAN FACTORIES INVOLVED IN THE A300B

The following list provides an overview of the MBB and VFW-Fokker factories involved in the Airbus project in the beginning, and their work packages.

Augsburg
Production of structural components

Bremen
Installation of all movable components in the wings

Donauwörth
Production of cabin doors, ribs, and flaps

Einswarden
Shaping of large metal sheets and production of fuselage shells

Hamburg
Structural assembly and fabrication of major components of the fuselage structure. From 1975 onward, complete outfitting of the empty "green" cabins of A300Bs flown from Toulouse to Hamburg.

Laupheim
Fabrication of plastic parts for cabin paneling, luggage racks, and air-conditioning system

Lemwerder
Modifications, cabin and component overhaul

Stade
Production of fuselage section 18, cargo hold and passenger doors

Varel
MBB machining center. Manufacture of components by milling to the desired shape.

An order by Thai Airways in 1977, initially for four A300B4s, ended an eighteen-month order drought, which had it lasted longer would undoubtedly have meant the end for Airbus. The Thai color scheme looks very nice on the aircraft. *MBB*

CHAPTER 7
AFTER THE CONTRACTS ARE SIGNED
SPARE-PARTS SUPPLY AND TRAINING

When the flurry of press photographer camera flashes dies away and the ink on the sales contract for a new aircraft type has dried, the real work begins for the airline and manufacturer—out of the limelight. Most sales contracts, especially for a new type, also include agreements on the necessary training of airline personnel in how to operate the new type, plus its spare-parts supply during future flight operations. This was also true in the early 1970s, when Airbus Industrie began negotiations with the first potential customers. The was great skepticism among the airlines as to whether Airbus was capable, not just of delivering new aircraft to its customers but also of providing all customary services for its future use. But the Airbus managers knew that they could count on their partners.

AIRSPARES

In the 1960s, the Hamburger Flugzeugbau GmbH had organized a global spare-parts supply system for its Hansa Jets at its Hamburg location, which operated around the clock, 365 days a year. The manufacturer maintained not just a hotline and parts warehouse at the company's seat in Hamburg, but also a branch in the United States. HFB's experience with the Hansa Jet thus gave it valuable experience in the development and production of jets, as well as their customer service, which predestined Hamburg as the location of the Airbus spare-parts division established in 1973. To this day, the Airbus Industrie Airspares Support and Services GmbH is not located in Finkenwerder, but on the outskirts of the Hamburg airport in the district of Großborstel, right next to the home of Lufthansa Technik on the famous Weg bei Jäger, and is responsible for supplying customers worldwide with original Airbus components and parts from the supplier industry. Analogous to HFB times, the airlines can count on routine spare-parts deliveries, but also on the express delivery of necessary parts after making contact with the Aircraft On-Ground Desk following unplanned technical problems with their Airbus aircraft, twenty-four hours a day, seven days a week, 365 days a year.

Whether at the Lufthansa hub in Frankfurt (1), in Asia (2), or in North America (3), since the first days of Airbus, Industrie Airbus customers have been supplied with spare parts around the clock, 365 days a year. The foundation for the present-day spare-parts logistics was laid by the Hamburger Flugzeugbau GmbH in the 1960s with the HFB 320. *Dr. John Provan / Airbus*

An internal paper by the Hamburg Division of Messerschmitt-Bölkow-Blohm GmbH (September) dated June 14, 1971, describes the approach to this challenge. There was, however, a big difference in supplying the forty-seven Hansa Jets—primarily used as business jets with low flying hours—with spare parts as compared to hundreds of wide-body airliners that transport thousands of passengers daily. From the start of the project, therefore, the planners of the Airspares Aircraft Spares Support Center Hamburg, which was begun and initially operated by MBB, recommended that the project be run as a separate business in order to achieve a clear separation of accounts from production. When Airspares was launched, it was assured that not only parts produced by the Airbus partners themselves would be stockpiled, but also those from countless external suppliers, so as to be able to cover all areas of the aircraft.

AÉROFORMATION

Parallel to Airspares, in 1973 an Airbus training center called Aéroformation, established the previous year, began operating in Toulouse. By the end of the 1980s, 35,000 Airbus students had received their type certifications on the A300B, A310, and A300-600—as pilots, copilots, cabin and maintenance personnel—at the Airbus subsidiary company Aéroformation. From the beginning, the training center had an A300B flight simulator, whose cockpit was made by LMT Simulation in France in cooperation with CAE Electronics of Canada and could move in all 6 degrees of freedom. The color displays were provided by the Link Division of the American Singer Company, whose very simple Link Trainer of the 1930s became synonymous with flight training. Even the first prospective pilots of the postwar Lufthansa completed their first hours of training in this crude simulator. In addition to the moving flight simulator, Aéroformation procured a static cockpit trainer, whose layout was 100 percent identical to the original and with whose help crews could familiarize themselves with the arrangement of instruments and controls. The so-called system trainer also familiarized prospective A300 pilots and flight engineers with the arrangement and operation of switches and levers.

Since delivery of the first production aircraft, the global Airbus spare-parts supply system has ranged from components for regular maintenance events, such as a D check on an A300B4 (*photo*) to urgently needed parts for unplanned repairs—so-called AOG cases (Aircraft on Ground). *Lufthansa*

CHAPTER 8
BREAKTHROUGH IN AMERICA
EVERY BEGINNING IS HARD

In the business year 2017, Airbus was able to book orders for 1,109 airliners and deliver 718, which were produced at the four final-assembly locations in Toulouse, Hamburg, Tainjin in China, and Mobile, Alabama, in the United States. Airbus was thus at home in the most-important commercial aviation markets on three continents. By July 2018, Airbus had received contracts for 18,397 aircraft, broken down into 816 A300/A310s, 14,276 A318/319/320/321 narrow-fuselage aircraft, 2,874 A330/A340/A350 wide-body jets, and 331 A380 megaliners. Not included in these numbers are the A220 regional jets, which Airbus has marketed under its own name since July 2018, after acquiring a majority of shares in the former Bombardier C-Series program, and are built at Mirabel in Canada, near Montreal.

The mothers and fathers of the Airbus program could only have dreamed of these imposing numbers and facts in the 1960s and 1970s. After Franz Josef Strauß, chairman of the board, and Henri Ziegler, Airbus president, launched Airbus Industrie as an economic-interest grouping according to French law on December 18, 1970, its managers hoped for sales of 1,100 Airbus A300s by the year 1980. If the A310 is included, the actual sales figure of 816 aircraft is not that far off. But the path—even to these, by comparison with 2018, very modest expectations—was a rocky one. When the A300B1 prototype took to the air for the first time on October 28, 1972, there was only the politically motivated order from the French national airline Air France for six A300B2s—after the Spanish airline Iberia had placed an order for four A300B4s in 1972 but then canceled it. At the end of 1974, by which time the A300B2 had been in airline service for eleven months, just fifty-three aircraft including options had been purchased. The orders trickled in, until in 1975 a slack period began, which went down in Airbus history as the "black period." For a period of eighteen months, Airbus unsuccessfully sought to find new customers for the A300B. As a result, production had to be scaled back drastically to half an aircraft per month. Critics demanded abandonment of the Airbus idea, which many saw as a failure, and that no more money be invested in an unprofitable project. But they had not reckoned on Roger Béteille, Bernard

Airbus Industrie opened the North American market in 1977 by leasing four A300B2s to Eastern Air Lines. *Airbus*

Lathière, and Felix Kracht and Airbus Industrie's chairman of the board Strauß, who had no intention of giving up, instead regarding the crisis as incentive for even-more-intensive sales efforts. These efforts were rewarded in May 1977 with an order for four A300B4s from the Asian airline Thai Airways International.

EASTERN AIRLINES:

THE FIRST AMERICAN CUSTOMER

Much more significant, however, was the possible breakthrough into the American commercial aviation market, of which there were signs in 1977. Tradition-rich but financially weak American Air Lines was looking for an economical replacement for its already-dated Boeing 727 jets, which operated on the dense route network on the American East Coast between Florida in the South and Massachusetts in the North. The deal, which opened the way for Airbus into the then largest commercial aviation market in the world, was for four A300B2s, which Eastern leased cost-free for six months from Airbus Industrie Leasing Corporation. If the airline was not satisfied with the aircraft, it could return the A300s to Airbus—or purchase them if satisfied. So that this transaction did not turn into a financial debacle for Airbus, the manufacturer hedged its bets by way of a sale of the aircraft to the Bank of America, from which Airbus immediately rented back the A300s and gave them to Eastern. The only costs for which Eastern was responsible were to have Airbus equip the cabin to its specifications—but even this expenditure was to be refunded by Airbus should the deal fall through. Eastern also ordered a flight simulator to retrain former Boeing 727 crews on the A300, and it could also have withdrawn from this contract within six months with no additional costs.

The first aircraft, with the registration N204EA, was delivered by Airbus to the United States in August 1977, while the remaining three examples arrived by the end of the year. The four A300B4s underwent their first major test during the peak season around Christmas 1977, when the sun-hungry inhabitants of the northern part of the country flew to sunny Florida on Eastern jets. With their 229 of a theoretically possible 345 seats, the four Airbuses, called A300 Whisperliners by Eastern, had comfortable seating.

The transaction did not take place without political differences between the United States and Europe, however, after the A300 was not permitted to use either the airport near the city of Washington, DC, or New York's La Guardia Airport with an economical takeoff and landing weight. The irrational reason given for the former was that quiet wide-body jets were not generally permitted to serve what is now the Ronald Reagan Airport in Washington—and the latter after doubts by the airport authority that La Guardia's taxiways and runways, which were built on supports in the water, would not be able to bear the weight of the A300. French politicians in particular regarded this as politically motivated sabotage of Airbus's imminent success in the United States. Before the matter could escalate further, Airbus Industrie and the Port Authority of New York agreed to reinforce the supports and allow an increase of the A300B2's maximum-allowable takeoff weight at La Guardia to about 297,624 pounds. This was sufficient to enable the Eastern Whisperliner to operate profitably.

Servicing a Pan Am A300B4 at Frankfurt. *Dr. John Provan*

NEW HOPE IN PAN AM

Airbus could breathe a sigh of relief when, on April 6, 1978, Eastern Air Lines signed a sales contract for twenty-three firm orders and nine options for the A300B4 with increased takeoff weight. Also incorporated were two A300B2s not accepted by Iran Air. The four leased A300B2s remained in the fleet by way of an extended lease, and in 1982, Eastern became the biggest customer of this aircraft type, with thirty A300s in service. Airbus was not content with this, of course, and it tried to secure follow-up orders from US airlines as quickly as possible. At first, however, it was limited to leasing A300s to the small airlines Capitol Air and Northeastern International Airways. In the summer of 1984, Capitol leased an A300B4 from Hapag-Lloyd Flug, while Northeastern leased two A300B2s each from Airbus and Lufthansa.

Boeing foiled the large contracts Airbus hoped to receive from United Airlines and Trans World Airlines with a counteroffer for its newly developed and somewhat smaller 767. The champagne corks did not pop again in Toulouse until September 13, 1984, when Pan American signed a memorandum of understanding for twelve Airbus A310-200s and sixteen A320s. Pending delivery of the new aircraft, Pan Am leased twelve A300B4s from Airbus, which as unsold "white tails" were mothballed at the Airbus factory in Toulouse in anticipation of better times. Pan Am placed its first A300B4 in service on December 23, 1984, followed by the first A310 on May 28, 1985. While their big sisters were primarily operated on Pan Am's domestic American network of routes, until German reunification its A310-200s operated on the Intra German Services routes between West German cities and West Berlin. The contract for the sixteen A320 medium-range jets was never finalized due to Pan Am's financial troubles.

With its A310-300s, the airline founded by Juan T. Trippe, once one of the most important in the world, gradually began replacing the larger Boeing 747-100 on routes from New York's John F. Kennedy International Airport (JFK) to European destinations. But even the economical Airbuses could not prevent the demise of the tradition-rich company. And so it was an A310-300 that on April 3, 1991, was the airline's last aircraft to leave London-Heathrow airport for New York after the financially troubled Pan Am sold its North Atlantic division to United Airlines. That was forty-five years after the first Pan American World Airways Lockheed L-049 Constellation had landed at London-Heathrow.

IMAGE IN DANGER

Continental Airlines, then based in Houston, maintained a considerable A300B4 fleet, with up to twenty-three aircraft, until 1986. It included aircraft purchased new from Airbus, purchased via Airbus on the secondhand market, and acquired from Eastern Air Lines, which went bankrupt in 1991. Like Continental it was part of the business empire of Frank Lorenzo. His business policy, which focused strongly on reducing costs, may have contributed to the A300 earning a bad reputation among travelers during its service with Continental because of constant technical problems and resultant canceled flights.

The American accident investigation authority, the National Transportation Safety Board (NTSB), found that pilot error, not negligent maintenance, was the cause of the crash of an A300-605R of American Airlines shortly after taking off from JFK airport in New York on November 12, 2001. With thirty-five examples, American was the biggest customer for the more developed A3000-600R version when AA 587 took off bound for Santo Domingo in

In addition to A300B4s, Pan Am also operated a fleet of A310-200s and 300s. The "billboard" paint finish introduced by Pan Am with delivery of the Airbus A300 and A310 was an example for many other airlines. *Airbus*

the Dominican Republic that day. Two minutes after takeoff, the A300-600R flew through turbulence caused by vortices from a preceding Boeing 747. The copilot, who was flying the aircraft, increased thrust to compensate and five times in rapid succession applied full rudder. The resulting overload caused the vertical tail, which was not designed to withstand such massive loads, to break off, and seconds later the by-then-uncontrollable aircraft crashed into the ground. All 260 persons onboard and five on the ground died in the crash.

American stuck with its A300-600Rs after this accident, the second worst involving a commercial aircraft in American history. According to the accident report, the aircraft's design bore no responsibility. The last aircraft did not leave the fleet until September 10, 2009, after twenty-one years of service. American had initially ordered twenty-five aircraft but later turned its options for ten more A300-600Rs into firm orders. The aircraft were used mainly on high-traffic-volume routes in the Caribbean, Central America, and the northern countries of South America.

CANADIAN A310S

American Airlines and Pan Am remained the only two American customers for brand-new A310s and A300-600s. The balance sheet was not quite as bleak, however, if one looked at the entire North American market, including Canada. Canadian aviation pioneer Max Ward had founded the airline Wardair, which he named after himself, and it was the first North American airline to order the A310-300, placing an order for fourteen aircraft of this type in March 1981. Only twelve were delivered before the airline merged with Canadian Airlines International in 1989. In addition to the A310s, Wardair operated three A300B4s leased from South African Airways from 1986 to 1989. Wardair was active both as a charter and line operator, before, in 1989, it was completely taken over by Canadian Airlines and its brand name disappeared. Since Canadian was already a Boeing 767 customer, the former Wardair A310s never flew in its colors.

The Canadian Armed Forces purchased five of the now-surplus Airbus A310-300s, which in 1992 and 1993 were converted into four CC-150 Polaris combi freighters and one VIP aircraft for use by the Canadian government. In 2008, two of the combi freighters were converted into Multi Role Tanker Transports, or MRTTs, by Airbus, to the same standard as the MRTTs flown by the German air force, which have since also been used as aerial-refueling aircraft. A Polaris MRTT can carry up to 39.6 tons of fuel over a distance of 2,858 miles for aerial refueling or, alternatively, accompany four CF-18 Hornets of the Royal Canadian Air Force as a flying gas station, nonstop from Canada to Europe.

Another Canadian A310-300 operator is Air Transat, based in Montreal, which at times has operated a mixed fleet of up to fourteen aircraft—and in 2018 was still operating seven aircraft of this type. All the aircraft were obtained on the used-aircraft market and had once been delivered new to Air Afrique, Condor, Emirates, Lufthansa, Wardair, and TAP Air Portugal. In July 2017, Air Transat signed an agreement with the aircraft-leasing company AerCap for the long-term lease of ten A321neo LR (long range) aircraft to replace its dated A310s, which in August 2018 had an average age of more than twenty-eight years. Deliveries of the 199-seat aircraft to replace the A310-300s, with their 250 seats, began in the spring of 2019. In June 2018, this agreement was supplemented by two A321neo and five A321neo LR aircraft, which are to replace the A330s when their leasing agreements expire between 2020 and 2022.

BREAKTHROUGH IN AMERICA 87

One of four CC-150 Polaris MRTT Multi Role Tanker Transports of the Royal Canadian Air Force, refueling two CF-18 Hornets. *Royal Canadian Air Force*

CHAPTER 9
THE A300 MODELS

A300B1

THE PROTOTYPES

After the successful first flight on October 28, 1972, Airbus Industrie sent the two A300B1 prototypes and the first two A300B2 production aircraft into flight testing. At the same time, static tests were carried out on components of an A300 delivered by European producers under the direction of the Centre d'Essais Aéronautiques de Toulouse flight test center. These included the aircraft's fuselage, wings, tail section, and flight controls. They were augmented by mockups of the undercarriage, the cockpit and cabin windows, the engine mounts, and engines, which were not of importance to the planned tests. For the fatigue tests prescribed by the certification authorities, the aircraft was divided into four sections and investigated for fatigue, breakage resistance, and crack formation behavior at the three German locations. Tests on the forward fuselage and tail section were carried out by VFW in Bremen, the fuselage center section and wings were tested by MBB at Munich-Ottobrunn, and MBB at Hamburg-Finkenwerder brought the aft fuselage to its expected load limits. Although the investigations concentrated on certain structural areas, parts of the fuselage sections directly in front of or behind them were installed to achieve optimal test results. In a first phase the program consisted of 96,000 simulated flights, until the tests to investigate the formation of cracks were extended to 120,000 virtual flights.

In addition to these experiments on static Airbus components, from August 1972, two months prior to the first flight, ONERA in Toulouse conducted vibration tests on prototype number 1. The object of these experiments, which were carried out with an aircraft weight of 113.5 tons at first, then 145.5 tons, was to recognize and if necessary eliminate at this early stage the spread of vibrations through the aircraft structure and the damage they might cause. The vibrating table was made to vibrate at a maximum frequency of 40 hertz by 250 springs bearing the A300's main undercarriage

Following conversion into a passenger aircraft, the second A300B1 prototype was flown by TEA of Belgium. *MBB*

and 70 springs to support the nose gear. The effects on the aircraft structure were collected by 586 probes attached to the fuselage, wings, and tail.

Parallel to the certification tests on the ground, four aircraft completed the prescribed certification program in the air. Construction number 1, with the French registration F-WUAB, was assisted by the second A300B1 prototype, with the registration F-WUAC, and the two A300B2s (F-WUAD and F-WUAA). The latter, which on November 20, 1973, became the first Airbus to enter service, was already largely up to series standard, after the first results of flight testing were incorporated in the form of minor adjustments. The A300B1 differed from the production model mainly in its fuselage, which was 8.7 feet shorter compared to the production version and had a lower maximum takeoff weight, which was reduced by 5.5 tons, to 137 tons. At first glance the prototypes could be recognized by the absence of the single windows of the B2 and B4 versions aft of the rear passenger doors.

Even before it was certified for airline service, in September 1973 Airbus sent the first prototype, now registered F-OCAZ, on a major sales tour through North, Central, and South America. Even though this tour did not lead to any direct orders, the A300 did convincingly demonstrate its reliability, since apart from a minor problem with one of its two CF6-50 power plants, there are no entries in the technical logbook. From the view of the Airbus sales people, the second tour, begun at Toulouse on December 31, 1973, was more successful. The trip, with stops in Athens, Tehran, Karachi, Delhi, Bombay, Amsterdam, and Belgrade, may have contributed to Olympic Airways, Iran Air, Pakistan International, and Air India signing contracts for Airbus aircraft in the years that followed.

The certification team's efforts were finally rewarded on March 15, 1974. The A300B became the first aircraft type ever to receive its German and French type certifications simultaneously. The four aircraft used for certification flew a combined 1,585 flying hours.

The A300B2's certification program for category III instrument landings began on April 1, 1974, and ended successfully in the midst of the autumn foggy season on September 30.

The A300B was thus certified and the test fleet could be taken out of service in stages. The first A300B1 prototype, with the registrations F-WUAB and F-OCAZ, was taken out of service in August 1974, while the first A300B2, with the registration F-WUAD and later F-BUAD, remained in service with Airbus for future developments. The second A300B2, with the registration F-WUAA, was equipped with a passenger cabin by the manufacturer after it was sold to the French domestic airline Air Inter. The second A300B1 prototype, with the registration F-WUAC, remained an exotic for many years after it was sold to the Belgian charter airline Trans European Airways (TEA) as ATLAS-TEF, and henceforth operated on the company's routes to sun destinations in the Mediterranean.

Unfortunately too late for the A300B1, Airbus recognized its history's importance to the future of the company, which in summer 2018 was expressed by a museum island with a Hansa Jet, Super Guppy, Transall, and Noratlas, as well as support for the Ein HANSA JET für Hamburg group in the Hamburg-Finkenwerder factory and the Aeroscopia Aviation Museum in Toulouse. The A300 with the registration F-WUAB displayed in the latter is not the original aircraft; rather, it is a B4 version originally built for Pan Am, which the museum painted in the historical colors of the prototype.

Neither of the two original A300B1s has survived, after TEA withdrew its aircraft from service in 1990, and for three decades it sat rotting on the outskirts of the Belgian capital's airport before it was scrapped. Even an appeal to Airbus management in Toulouse by aviation enthusiasts, urging it to become aware of its history and save this unique piece of the company's history, went unheard in the 1990s. The second A300B1, originally registered F-WUAB, did not fare much better. A section of its fuselage a few meters long and parts of its wings can be seen in the Deutsches Museum in Munich.

THE A300 MODELS   91

The A300B2-320 version for SAS incorporated more than 400 detail changes, including two Pratt & Whitney JT9D engines. They were so tailored to the Scandinavian airline's needs that it had a difficult time finding buyers for the relatively new jets after just a few years of service. *SAS*

A300B2

THE FIRST PRODUCTION MODEL

The A300B2 was certified in March 1974, and to Air France went the honor of the first scheduled use of this new type on the Paris-to-London route on May 23, 1974. The first six Airbuses accepted by Lufthansa, beginning in February 1976, were also B2 models, with which the German airline joined a circle of international customers such as Air Siam of Thailand, Eastern Airlines in the United States, Indian Airlines, Iran Air, South African Airways, and Toa Domestic Airlines of Japan. The four A300B2-320s built for Scandinavian Airlines System (SAS) were surely the most-unusual examples of this type. Airbus president Roger Béteille and SAS director Knut Hagrup signed an initial sales contract in Stockholm for two firm orders and ten options, of which only two led to firm orders for the A300B2-320.

The aircraft, tailored for the northern Europeans, had no fewer than 400 comprehensive changes compared to the basic model offered by Airbus. Not only was SAS the first customer for the Pratt & Whitney JT9D-59A power plant, offered as an alternative by Airbus, it also wanted a version with features of both the A300B2 and B4 versions, with longer range and increased takeoff weight—but without the central fuel tank. This resulted in an aircraft with a range of 2,237 miles, which after the installation of another fuel tank during its service life was increased to a maximum of 2,610 miles. Other extras that differed from the A300B standard were more-powerful brakes on the main undercarriage, larger cargo-hold doors (which made it possible to load Boeing 747– and McDonnell Douglas DC-10–compatible containers), and an alternative flight control system in the cockpit. The passenger cabin also differed from that of the standard Airbus, after SAS cabin crews had an important say in the layout of the aircraft and requested a spatial separation between the catering zones and the five washrooms to accelerate service delivery onboard. This required a complex and therefore not very successful transfer of supply lines for the kitchens and toilets beneath the cabin floor, which during the service life of the aircraft frequently led to leaks and premature structural damage caused by leaking fluids.

Selection by the KSSU Consortium

Decades before the air carrier alliances that are now common, Swissair and SAS began combining the selection, definition, and maintenance of their fleets. In 1957, the two airlines established their alliance when they ordered the Douglas DC-8 long-range jet, followed by the SE 210 Caravelle, Convair 900 Coronado, and Douglas DC-9. When the jumbo age arrived toward the end of the 1960s, SAS, Swissair, and KLM faced the challenge of operating and maintaining a few examples of what was then considered a gigantic aircraft in a way that made sense economically. This led in 1968 to the signing of the KSS (KLM/SAS/Swissair) agreement, which defined common technical and operational standards for this aircraft. Within this framework, SAS assumed responsibility for overhauling the Pratt & Whitney JT9D engines at its Stockholm Linta workshops, while KLM conducted D checks on its partners' aircraft in Amsterdam. The 747 fleet's APUs were maintained by the French company UTA, which joined the trio of airlines in February 1970. One year earlier the partners had been able to agree on the definition of the McDonnell Douglas DC-10 long-range jet, which had been ordered by all four airlines. When SAS ordered the A300B2 in 1977, the KSSU partners had already presented the technical specification, on whose basis the Scandinavians signed their order, becoming the only one of the four airlines to buy the A300.

Although Swissair was a member of the KSSU consortium, it worked with Lufthansa on the conception of the A310. *ETH-Bibliothek Zurich, Swissair*

Iran Air was an early Airbus customer, and in 1978 it began operating A300B2s (*photo*). These were later supplemented by A300B4s, A300-600s, and A310s. In the summer of 2018 an A300B2 sister aircraft to EP-IBV, seen here, was still in service with Air Iran. *Lufthansa*

Despite this, this aircraft type was no newcomer to the KSSU airlines, since major overhauls of Thai Airways International's fleet of A300B4s were carried out at Stockholm-Arlanda by its parent company SAS. During so-called D checks, KLM overhauled the General Electric CF6-50 engines of the Thai machines in Amsterdam on the basis of a subcontract, while at the same time the French company UTA serviced the APUs in Paris.

Planned

The Flying Vikings' joy over their new Airbus A300s was short lived. After a change of strategy at the beginning of the 1980s that favored the smaller DC-9 on many of the flights spread over the day, instead of fewer flights by the big A300, SAS transferred its Airbuses to its charter subsidiary Scanair. Prior to this, MBB converted all four aircraft to A300B4 standard, with a central fuel tank. The A300's range was still inadequate, especially on the longest routes from Sweden to the Canary Islands, to the frustration of the vacationers, who often could not take all their luggage with them. There was a saying among Scanair employees: "When an A300 flies to the Canaries, a DC-8 has to follow with the baggage." A sale of the unpopular aircraft initially seemed impossible, since the 400 special changes requested by SAS in 1977 had made the SAS Airbuses into exotics in any existing Airbus fleet. After the loss of one aircraft during its lease to Malaysia Airlines, SAS finally succeeded in selling its remaining three Airbuses to the Danish charter operator Conair of Scandinavia. The aircraft later flew with the Scandinavian airline Premiair and Bosporus European Airways of Turkey. All three surviving A300B2-320s were still in existence in the summer of 2018, at a small aircraft graveyard on the outskirts of the Istanbul airport, where they faced an uncertain future.

A300B4

THE SUCCESS MODEL

The first example of the A300B4, which from 1974 until into the 1980s was regarded as the standard Airbus model, was not procured by one of the large airlines operating around the world, but rather by a small West German charter airline by the name of Germanair. Not to be confused with the airline of the same name that forms part of the Lufthansa group in the new millennium, the first German airline with this name was established in 1964 in Baden-Baden as Südwestflug. The company was purchased by Munich building contractor Jörg Schörghuber in 1970. After the BAC 111, the A300B4 was the second jet operated by the company on routes to tourist destinations on the Mediterranean. Germanair's first A300B4-2C had originally been ordered by the Spanish airline Iberia as one of four aircraft in January 1972—however, the entire order was canceled several months later. Thus tiny Germanair had the honor of being the first airline anywhere in the world to fly the A300B4. This Airbus, registered D-AMAX, was followed on February 20, 1978, by a second aircraft, with the registration D-AMAP. After Schörghuber combined Bavaria Fluggesellschaft, which was also part of his group of companies, with Germanair to form Bavaria-Germanair in 1977, this A300B4 was delivered by Airbus in the new colors of the merger partner. In January 1979, the Munich building speculator sold his airline to the tourism company Hapag-Lloyd, based at Hanover-Langenhagen airport—which until then had flown its Boeing 727s to tourist destinations. In contrast to Bavaria-Germanair's BAC 111s, the two A300B4s did not remain in its fleet for just a short time; instead they were joined by seven more aircraft of the same type. They formed the backbone of the Hapag-Lloyd fleet in the 1980s. They were replaced

The German charter airline Condor used both A300B4s (*photo*) and A310s on its network of routes to vacation destinations. *Condor*

Germanair, which in 1977 merged with its sister company Bavaria to form Bavaria-Germanair, was the first German customer for an Airbus type. It placed its first A300B4, with the registration D-AMAX, in service on June 1, 1975—ten months before the first A300B2 entered service with Lufthansa. *Borgmann collection*

in the 1990s by five Airbus A310-200s and eight A310-300s, which after the company was renamed Hapagfly in 2005 remained in service in their blue paint scheme for a short time.

Hapag-Lloyd was the first customer for the A300C4 combi version of the A300B4, which was conceived by Airbus for use as a pure freighter or passenger jet, but also for mixed cargo-passenger flights. The first aircraft of this type was registered D-AHLB and flew for the first time on May 16, 1979. The brand-new aircraft was flown from Airbus in Toulouse to the MBB facility in Lemwerder for installation of the large cargo door on the main deck and a reinforced cabin floor. The conversion that was carried out can be seen as the forerunner of the program for converting used A300s and A310s into freighters, launched in the 1990s at the Elbe Flugzeugwerken in Dresden, and production of new A310F and A300-600F freighters. The A300C4 delivered to Hapag-Lloyd on January 31, 1980, was equipped with 315 seats, like the fleet's other passenger machines. The airline flew its first pure-freight charter flight to Africa in 1982. The flight from Cologne/Bonn to Lagos on January 23, with 45 tons of air freight, was also the first commercial use of a twin-jet, wide-body aircraft on a purely freight route.

THE FREIGHTERS: A SECOND LIFE

At the beginning of the 1990s Airbus recognized that there existed a worldwide market for economical and, in particular, quiet cargo aircraft with a capacity of 33 to 55 tons on midrange routes. The freighters then in use, converted airliners such as the Boeing 707, Douglas DC-8, Lockheed L-188 Electra, and even the piston-engined Douglas DC-6 from the 1950s were either too noisy, too uneconomical, or simply too old to have a future in the air freight market. On the other hand, the first A300B4s, built in the 1970s and now being retired from passenger service, still had about half their maximum-allowable flying hours remaining and thus had the prospect of continuing in service in the second half of their aircraft lives as freighters.

Airbus seized the opportunity in 1993 and, after an initial order from Federal Express, began converting used A300s and A310s from passenger aircraft into freighters at its Hamburg facility. Three years later, Airbus transferred this work package to the Elbe Fluggesellschaft GmbH (EFW) in Dresden, which at that time was a subsidiary of the German group DASA and in summer 2018 belonged to Airbus. From the beginning, original design data from the manufacturer and original parts from Airbus Industrie were exclusively used for these conversions. The first customer for the A300B4F was the express freight company DHL, and for the cargo version of the A310-200, the American company Federal Express.

In addition to converting passenger aircraft into freighters, called Passenger to Freighter (P2F) by Airbus, for the first time the manufacturer also offered an aircraft purpose built as a freighter, the A300-600F, whose largest customers were the express freight services UPS and FedEx. In the summer of 2018 UPS was still operating fifty-two A300F4-600R(F)s, all of which were new-build aircraft, while FedEx was flying sixty-eight converted A300-600(F) and A300-600R(F) freighters, as well as new-build A300F4-600Rs on its global network of routes.

THE A300 MODELS 99

View of the A300/A310 conversion building of the Elbe Flugzeugwerke in Dresden. *Elbe Flugzeugwerke*

DHL—the German postal service's express freight company—was one of the first customers for freighters converted from A300 passenger aircraft. *Elbe Flugzeugwerke*

Installation of a new cargo door on the main deck of a converted A310. *Elbe Flugzeugwerke*

102 AIRBUS A300/310

Federal Express was the first customer for A310 freighter conversions. *EADS EFW*

THE AIRBUS ELBE FLUGZEUGWERKE A300 AND A310 FREIGHTERS

Maximum Payloads	
A300B4-100F	99,208 pounds
A300B4-200F	97,885 pounds
A310-200F	89,508 pounds
A310-300F	88,405 pounds
A300-600RF	107,365 pounds

British Aerospace Aviation Services A300B4-200F

Although responsible for the design and manufacture of wings for all Airbus types, British Aerospace launched its own program for conversion of passenger aircraft into freighters to compete with Airbus. At Filton, its subsidiary BAe Aviation Services began producing conversion kits for turning A300B4 aircraft into freighters, and installed them in customers' aircraft on the spot. In contrast to EFW in Dresden, whose converted A300s and A310s were fitted with hydraulically operated cargo doors and newly made floor panels from the A300-600F, the cargo doors of the A300s modified by the British company could be operated electrically, and the floor structure was not new, only reinforced. The result in terms of payload was almost identical, however.

The first aircraft converted at Filton was an aircraft that had originally been ordered by Eastern Air Lines in 1980, and after conversion it was operated by the British freight line Channel Express. Another customer was Farnair of Switzerland. BAe Aviation Services also offered to bring the A300B4-100 version up to version 200 standard with a higher takeoff weight. BAe Aviation Services' conversion program was halted in 2002.

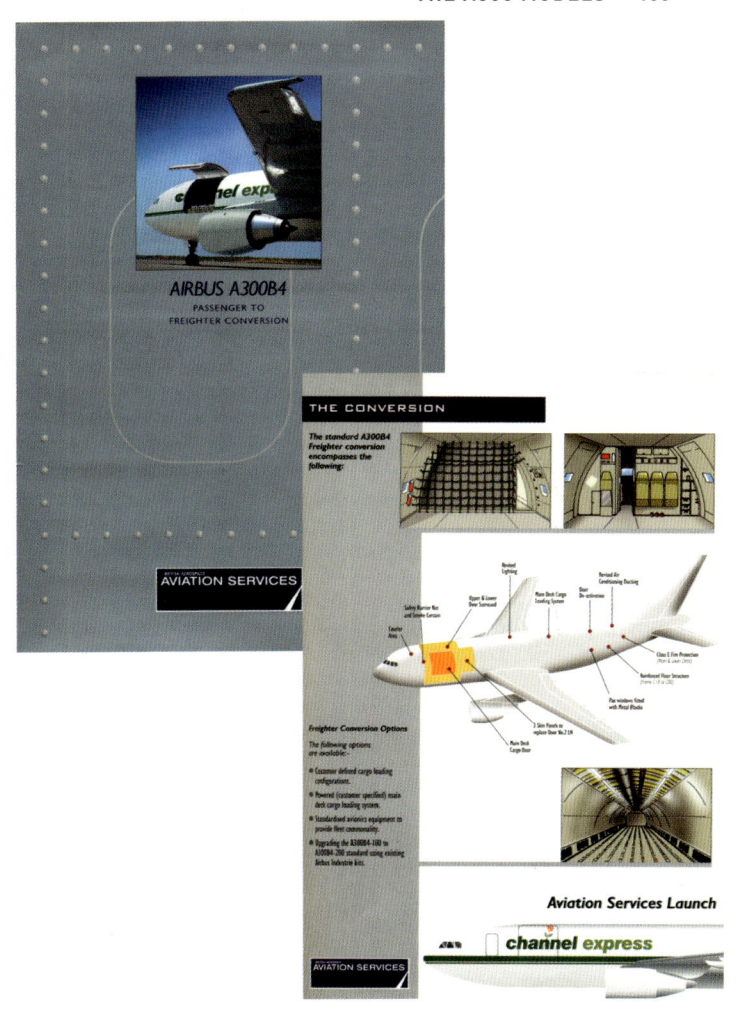

British Aerospace Aviation Services used this brochure to explain its concept for conversion of A300B passenger aircraft into freighters. *British Aerospace Aviation Services*

CHAPTER 10
THE SECOND GENERATION

A SERIES OF STUDIES AND ROUGH DESIGN CALCULATIONS LED US INTO THINKING THAT A GOOD RESULT COULD BE ACHIEVED ONLY BY USING A NEW TRANSONIC WING.

—Prof. Ernst Simon, on Lufthansa's participation in the A310 wing design

AIRBUS A310

Even before the A300B1 prototype made its first flight in 1972, it was the declared intention of the European aircraft manufacturer to develop an entire family of aircraft. Thus, following the prototype, the A300B2 and B4 models were produced. They were stretched by 8.7 feet, with higher takeoff weights, but otherwise were identical to the prototype. The version of the A300B1 with more-powerful CF6-50C engines, designated A300B3, was not produced, however. The proposed A300B5 and B6 freighters, based on the B1 and B4, and the A300B7, powered by Rolls-Royce RB 211 engines, which was offered to British European Airways, got no further than the drawing board. The same was true of the A300B8, with reduced engine power and takeoff weight, which was conceived for the North American market. After numerous design optimizations, the A300B9, B10, and B11 projects finally led to the A310 as well as the A330 and A340.

The A310 had its beginnings in the late 1970s. Swissair and Lufthansa played such a major role in its development that both airlines can claim that it was their technical work that launched this successful model. When the two airlines placed the first orders for the A310 in April 1979, three competing airliners—the Boeing 767, Boeing 757, and Airbus A310—were just becoming available. United Airlines took on the role of launch customer for the Boeing 767-200, and British Airways and Eastern Air Lines were the first to order the Boeing 757, successor to the smaller 727. The order by the British flag carrier, which was officially concluded between Boeing and the airline in March 1979, could not have come at a worse moment: at the same time, the British government was working to become an official partner of the Airbus consortium. Especially in France there were still memories of how the British partner had pulled out of the A300 project in 1969. That was at a time when the future of Airbus hung by a silken thread, and this decision came within a hair of ending the idea of a European wide-body jet. British Airways' interest in a competing American project reopened this old wound,

It was not until the very successful A310 (*photo*) and A300-600 models that the Airbus consortium really took off. *Lufthansa*

In the summer of 2018, Yemenia-Yemen Airways was flying one A310 and had previously operated five others. *Airbus*

With thirteen aircraft, Emirates, the airline of the United Arab Emirates, operates the largest A310 fleet in the region. *Emirates*

which had not healed, especially on the French side. The federal German Airbus partners saw the matter more calmly—not least because Lufthansa also ordered aircraft solely on the basis of what was best for the company, and strictly refused to accept political interference. After the British government succeeded in calming the French, on January 1, 1979, British Aerospace officially became a partner in the Airbus consortium and assumed a 20 percent share in the Airbus A310 project, as well as development of the wing for the new Airbus type.

The A310s flown by Hapag-Lloyd and Condor enjoyed great popularity in the German charter market. *Hapag Lloyd / TUIfly & Condor*

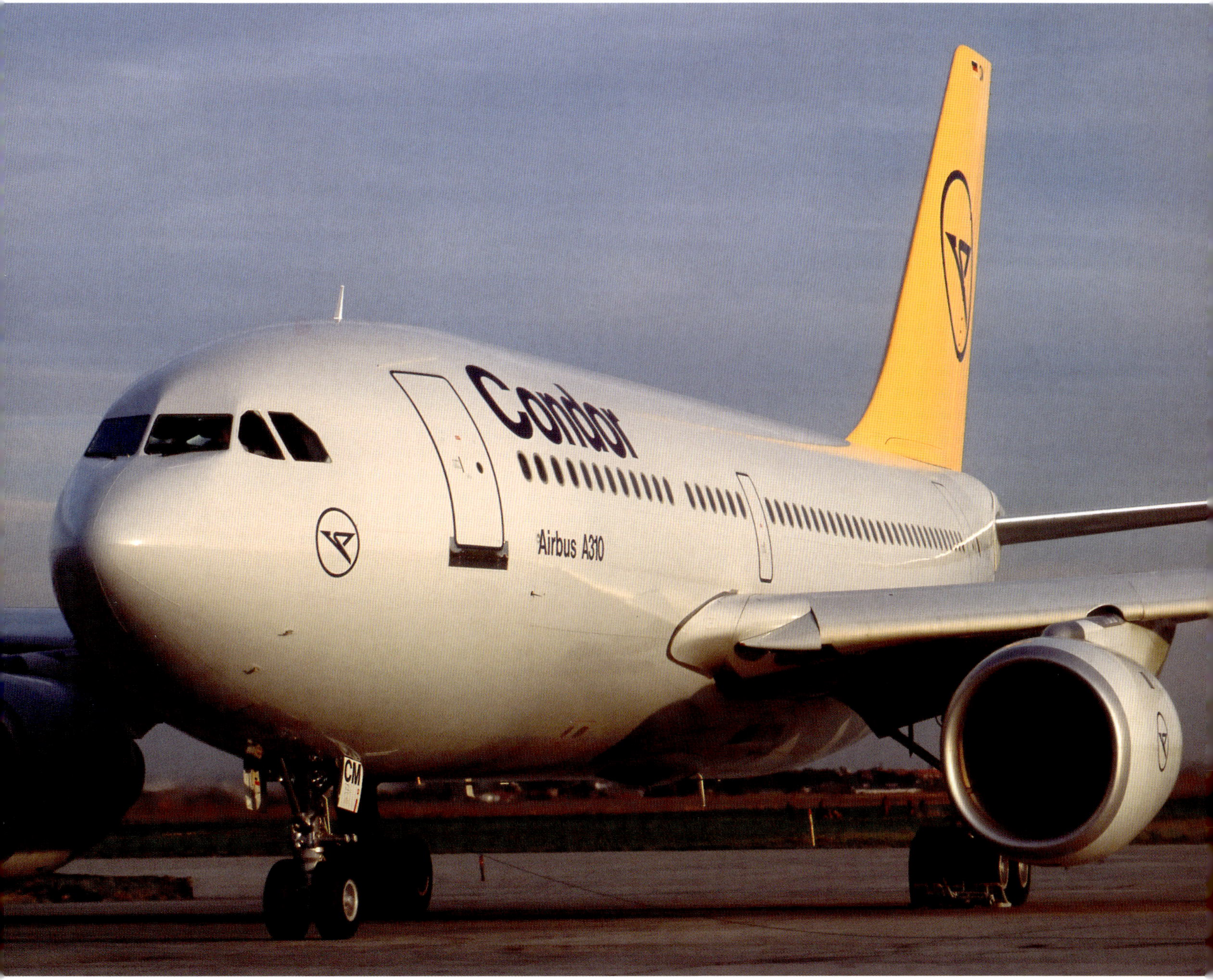
Condor
Airbus A310
CM

A310: THE LUFTHANSA JET

With a seating for about 200, in terms of capacity the 757/767/A310 are between the Boeing 727-200, at the lower end of the scale, and the larger A300. Analogous to the selection of the Boeing 737 in the 1960s, once again Lufthansa initially developed a midrange fleet concept for the 1980s before it selected one of the three types on offer. The fleet planners determined a requirement for two aircraft types for the 120–160 capacity ranges, and another two types for 210 to 270 seats. Without at first naming specific aircraft types, they believed that they could achieve this goal with two narrow-fuselage types, called types IA and IB, and two wide-body jets designated IIA and IIB. This concept of "flexibility at the lowest cost" presupposed the highest degree of relationship between the basic types in categories I and II, in order to keep their maintenance costs low for Lufthansa. In fact, the Boeing 737-230 Advanced and Boeing 727 Advanced illustrated the types IA and IB, while the A300B2/B4 corresponded to the type IIB. The search for the still-missing type IIA to complete the quartet ultimately led to the decision to purchase the A310. What wide-ranging consequences an aircraft purchase can have was outlined by Airbus president Bernard Lathière in his 1979 New Year's address to the staff. Perhaps with Lufthansa in mind, he spoke of those airlines that for many years were practically married to their American competitors and now faced the decision to let in a new and still-little-known maker. Lathière prophesied: "The people who make such decisions risk their jobs and the existence of their companies, for their choice has consequences for the next twenty years, as long as this aircraft type is in service with their airline. If the aircraft and customer service are not good, this means twenty years of failure." When the Lufthansa chief executive Dr. Herbert Culmann and board member Dipl.-Ing. Reinhardt Abraham signed a firm order for twenty-five aircraft and options for another twenty-five worth more than 1.5 billion deutsch marks on April 2, 1979, perhaps these words were ringing in their ears—and nevertheless they could be very sure that they were buying an aircraft tailored to meet their requirements. Professor Ernst Simon, longtime head of the Main Department Technical Projects and, in 1978, partly responsible for the selection of future Lufthansa types, described the start of the A310 program as follows: "Without the influence exerted by Lufthansa, the A310 would not have been built in its existing form. Airbus planned to build only a shortened version of the A300, which was envisaged by Lufthansa as the A310MC (minimum change). Even then, the old adage of aircraft construction—that while a shortened aircraft with fewer seats reduces return potential, operating costs remain almost the same—was true. With respect to the A310MC, that did not seem to us to be a good idea." Professor Simon found an ally at Airbus Industrie in Jean Roeder. Not only could he communicate with the Airbus head of development from Luxembourg in German, but both engineers spoke the same language when it came to their views on aircraft design:

The launching of an aircraft family with the A310, without which the A300-600 would not have been possible, and the step into the long-range market with the A340, which also made possible the A330, were fruits of our collaboration and remain cornerstones in the success of Airbus.

Lufthansa and Swissair designed the A310 cockpit, which for the first time had an electronic system for displaying primary flight data on display screens, in cooperation with Airbus Industrie. *ETH-Bibliothek Zurich, Swissair*

Against initial resistance from the Airbus sales people, who preferred development of a design that was as cost-efficient as possible, Roeder and Simon set to work on the concept of what from their point of view was the optimal A310 design. It included a new transonic wing, whose point of maximum thickness was far to the rear. This caused flow speed to build up gently and steadily—thus causing less drag and lower fuel consumption. The wings of the A310 were slimmer in outline than those of the A300, and, compared to its big sister, they were fitted with a simpler flap configuration, which reduced weight and was easier to service. With the spoilers developed by VFW in Bremen on the upper wing surface, the A310 was the first production aircraft in the world with carbon fiber components. Weight-reducing composite materials were also used in the control surfaces, the aircraft nose, the engine fairings, and the leading edges of the horizontal stabilizer. Also new were the wingtip plates—A310 wingtip fences in Airbus jargon—which reduced the formation of wingtip vortices and thus fuel consumption. These vertical mini wings, now standard in aircraft design, whose modern winglet or sharklet versions can be up to several meters tall depending on the aircraft type, had their premiere on a commercial aircraft with the A310-300.

The Lufthansa people under Simon's leadership became actively involved in the design phase of the A310 in January 1978. On average, ten engineers from Lufthansa's technical department—up to twenty at peak times—were permanently involved with the specification for the new aircraft. Four Lufthansa pilots were also actively involved in designing the cockpit layout, bringing their experience in the two-man operation of the Boeing 737 and the concept of the more modern 737 Advanced flight deck into the A310 team.

In addition to the aerodynamic adaptation of the wing and aft fuselage, the Lufthansa and Airbus engineers focused on development of a completely innovative two-man cockpit. Professor Simon recalled: "I didn't believe that I could sell the two-man cockpit to the pilots. But I was wrong. When in addition to Lufthansa, Swissair also declared its intention to order the aircraft, now called A310X by Airbus, the Swissair pilots declared themselves in agreement with the two-man cockpit concept, and the Lufthansa pilots followed their example."

In a paper defining the Airbus A310 cockpit, in December 1979 Lufthansa explained its motivation to participate in the development of the first so-called glass cockpit in a commercial aircraft. It stated: "The cockpit is the interface between an and technology in solving the task 'control of an aircraft.' This task is not characterized solely by the fact that man (the aircraft crew) must master the technology of the aircraft under all conditions. Instead he must primarily deal with conditions in the environment in which the aircraft is moving.

"Deutsche Lufthansa AG therefore strove to achieve a maximum of safety by exerting influence in the layout, especially of the cockpit, of the aircraft it operated (with particular focus on the area of the human-machine interface)."

For the first time, the use of then-new technologies, such as a modern flight management system in combination with first-generation screen displays, made it possible for both pilots to see and operate all control elements from the normal seated position during flight. This eliminated the need for a third person in the cockpit. The key feature of the new A310 cockpit was the concentration of system operation on a panel arranged above the heads of the two

Wingtip fences were at first an exclusive external feature of the A310-300 long-range version, but in the course of the program they were also offered for the A310-200. *ETH-Bibliothek Zurich, Swissair*

It was only after the intervention of the Lufthansa technical department that Airbus built an A310 entirely to the customer's taste. *Lufthansa*

pilots. In place of the usual indicator instruments, warning lights, and toggle switches, push switches were used in the A310 cockpit, which with the aid of two independent lighting options could indicate the switch position ON or OFF or a fault in the affected system. Monitoring of the engines was achieved mainly by analog instruments, as well as two screen displays on the center instrument panel in the pilots' field of view. When a fault occurred, a schematic representation of the system appeared automatically on the right of both displays, with the failed part in a contrasting color. In addition, in this presentation all of the system's current state values were displayed in digital and analog form. At the same time, the name of the failed system and an indication to the pilots in which sequence they had to correct the fault appeared on the left display. This represented a considerable reduction in workload compared to pure analog instrumentation.

The primary flight instruments for indicating the aircraft's attitude and position were shown on two screen displays, one each for the pilot and copilot. For the first time, using the aircraft's flight-path computer, the pilots could read the aircraft's actual position in a realistic map picture and calculate, indicate, and automatically fly its planned course. The A310's flight-path computer, in conjunction with the screen display of the electronic flight instruments, thus made a significant contribution to reducing pilot workload. The now-indispensable glass cockpit was born with the A310.

THE WAGER

I had known Joe Sutter for more than twenty years, and when he again began going on about the A310 with our chief technology officer Reinhardt Abraham, I said that I was ready to bet him that his claims would be proven wrong. He had no choice but to agree to the wager. It was put down in writing and signed by us both. He bet that the A310 would not achieve the promised specifications in at least two of the three important and precisely defined performance parameters. After completion of the A310 acceptance flights, I sent Joe Sutter the corresponding pages from our Performance Guarantees Compliance Document, in which performance figures measured under exact conditions were compared with the guaranteed values. The A310 had achieved the rated values in all respects, and Sutter was forced to pay his bet—it was a bottle of whiskey.

—Prof. Ernst Simon, on his wager with legendary Boeing engineer Joe Sutter, who became world famous as "Father of the 747"

THE SECOND GENERATION 115

The A310-300 in formation flight with its even more successful successor, the A320-200. *Lufthansa*

A300-600

THE BIG SISTER

Although it was essentially an A300, the A300-600 adopted many design features of its smaller sister the A310. It shared its glass cockpit; various aircraft systems; the modified, aerodynamically optimized tail shape, including a trim tank housed in the horizontal tail; and the later, more fuel-efficient power plants of the A310. A new feature, however, was the vertical tail produced at Stade near Hamburg, which for the first time on a jet airliner was made entirely of the stable and fracture-resistant composite material CFK. With the A300-600, Stade established itself as the venue of the black art, as the production of CFK was jokingly referred to on account of the black color of the basic material used to make components. In the summer of 2018, the factory in Stade was producing vertical-tail assemblies for the entire product line—from the A320ceo and A320neo families to the A330, the A350XWB to the A380, whose gigantic tail measures a record-breaking 46 feet.

For the first time in Airbus history, an airline based in the United States, American Airlines, became the first customer of one of its aircraft; however, the A300-600 is also very popular with airlines around the world. Of the 561 examples of all versions of the A300 built, Airbus has been able to sell 313 A300-600s alone—making it the most popular A300 model. Lufthansa also placed fifteen aircraft of this type into service within Germany and Europe and on flights to the Middle East and Africa between 1987 and 2009. Its ability to "shovel" passengers changing flights from destinations on the European continent to the international flights at the Lufthansa hub in Frankfurt has earned it the appropriate nickname "Cont-Shovel" (continental shovel) among Lufthansa personnel.

Brand-new and used A300-600s enjoyed great popularity, especially among express services, in the summer of 2018. Their use is described in the chapter titled "The A300 Models." The A300-600 base model was followed by the A300-600R (R = range), which was certified on March 10, 1988. Fully loaded, it can fly a distance of about 4,350 miles. American Airlines was also the first customer for the A300-600R version. Production of the A300 ended with the delivery of the last A300-600R built for Federal Express, with the construction number 878—twenty-five years after the maiden flight of the A300B1 prototype. The aircraft took to the air for the first time on April 18, 2007, and was delivered to FedEx on July 17, with the registration N692FE.

THE SECOND GENERATION 117

Lufthansa used its A300-600s primarily to fill its overseas flights from Frankfurt with connecting passengers. *Lufthansa*

The A300-600 was very popular, especially with Asian airlines such as Thai Airways, seen here. The airline had previously ordered the A300B4 in 1977. *Airbus*

A300-600s were still in service with Iran Air in the summer of 2018. *Airbus*

A300-600 Work Sharing

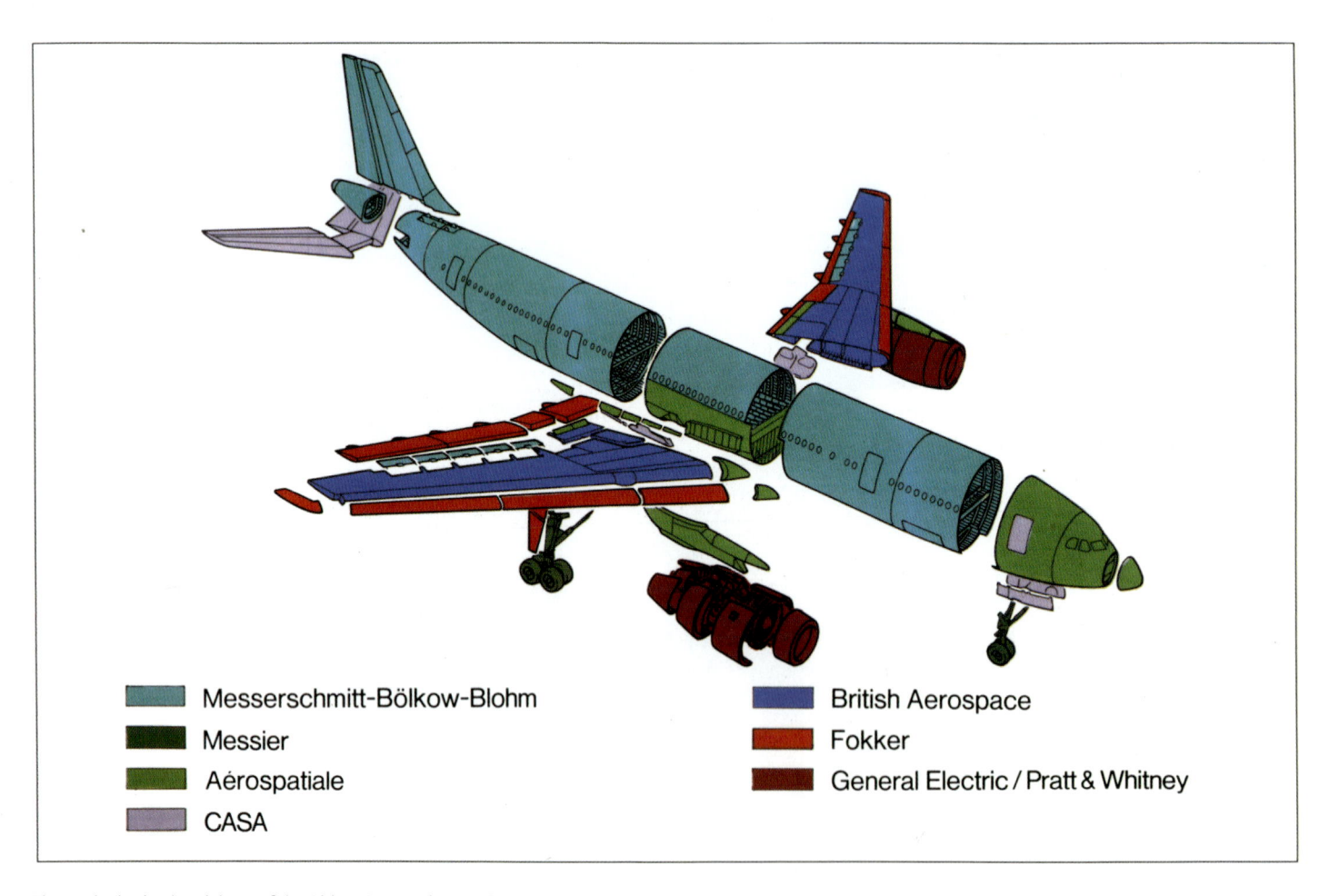

The work-sharing breakdown of the Airbus A310 and A300-600. *MBB*

A310 Work Sharing

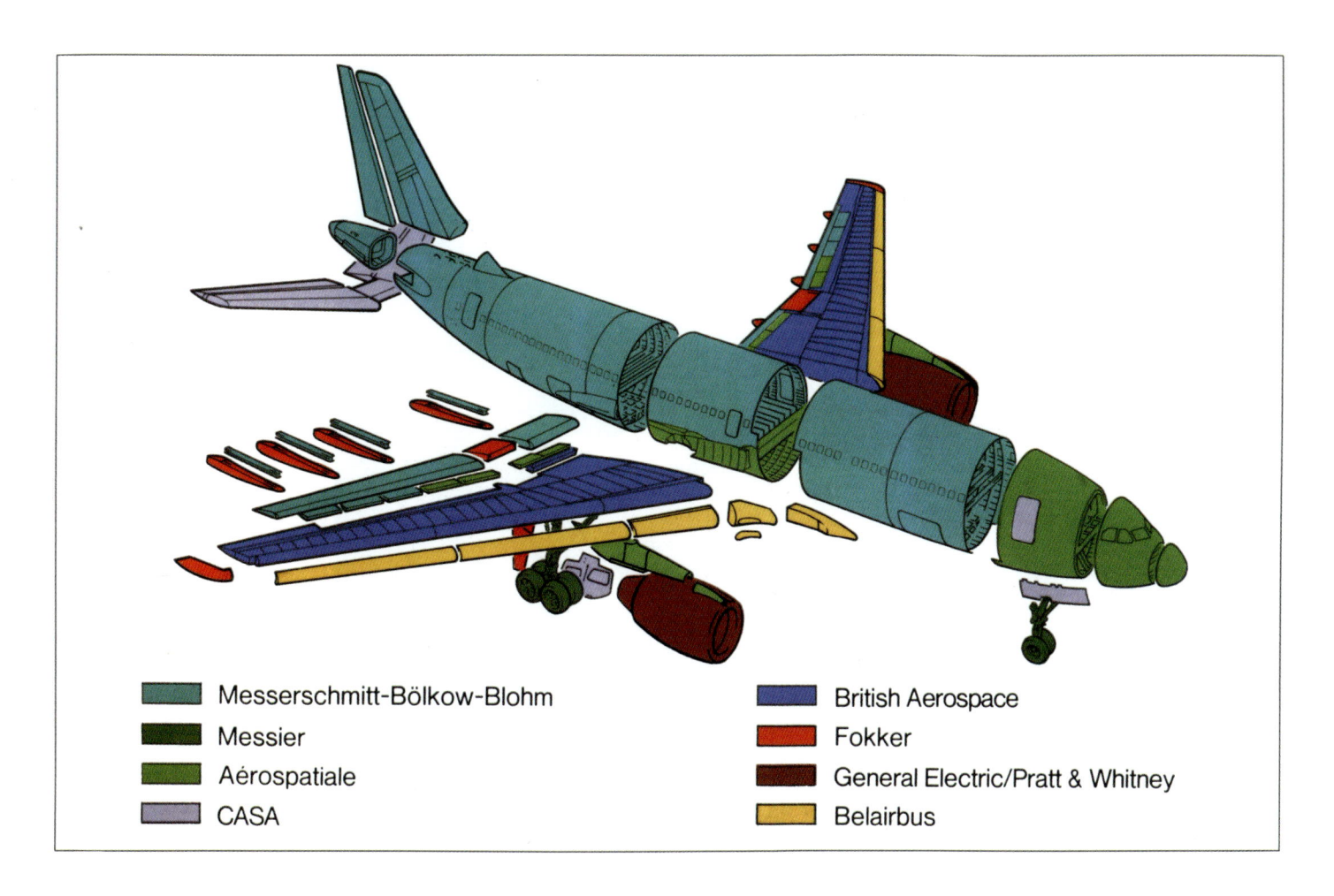

■	Messerschmitt-Bölkow-Blohm	■	British Aerospace
■	Messier	■	Fokker
■	Aérospatiale	■	General Electric/Pratt & Whitney
■	CASA	■	Belairbus

CHAPTER 11
LOGISTICAL CHALLENGE
ANSWERED BEFORE THE FIRST FLIGHT

AERO SPACELINES 377SGT

SUPER GUPPY TURBINE 201

In the beginning years of Airbus Industrie, Toulouse, France, was the consortium's sole final-assembly line. The major reason the location in the South of France was chosen was the combined know-how of the companies involved in production of the SE 210 Caravelle, while optimal conditions for test-flying could be expected in the moderate climate of southwestern France. After the project partners decided in the early planning stages that the European partner factories would produce complete fuselage sections and wings with systems already installed instead of small structural parts, the question of how this should take place remained to be answered. Shipment of Airbus components by sea would have been possible, both from Broughton in Great Britain on the Irish Sea, where the Airbus wings were made, and from Hamburg on the Elbe, from where large fuselage sections and the tail began their journey to France. Even the factory at Saint-Nazaire, on the French Atlantic coast, would have qualified for sea transport. The sticking point of this idea, however, was the inland location of Toulouse, which was reachable only by a combined transport by seagoing vessel / inland waterway vessel / truck, with the cargo having to be reloaded twice—and so this idea quickly left the heads of the logisticians. The other idea that was considered, transporting the large fuselage sections—18.4 feet in diameter—and the wings over the European road network, would have led to a permanent state of emergency on the transport arteries of Europe, which were not yet well developed at that time, and transport by rail was never considered because of the outsized components. This was quite apart from the risk that the sensitive components could easily have been damaged during ground transport. It is something that Boeing experiences to this day; the line from Wichita to Seattle, which delivers 737 fuselages to the final-assembly line in Seattle, is a popular target for weapons enthusiasts, who use the trains for target practice.

LOGISTICAL CHALLENGE 123

Without the use of the Super Guppy transports, the delivery of large Airbus components across Europe would have become an almost insurmountable logistical nightmare. *Borgmann collection*

The Aero Spacelines 377SGT Super Guppy Turbine 201 was originally developed to transport sections of NASA rockets to Florida for final assembly. NASA

By comparison, in Airbus use the fuselage sections of the A320 family look almost petite. *Borgmann collection*

Shipment by air thus seemed to Airbus to be the safest and fastest way of solving the pan-European logistics problem—but what aircraft was capable of performing this task? The answer to this burning question was provided by NASA, the American space agency, and its program of manned flights to the moon. NASA was also searching for a way of transporting components of the Saturn V rocket—assembled at various locations in the United States—to Florida for final assembly of the moon rockets.

Jack Conroy offered the solution to the transport problems. At the beginning of the 1960s, he and Lee Mansdorf had begun converting Boeing 377 Stratocruiser airliners and C-97s, their military equivalents, into freighters for large-volume loads. Their company Aero Spacelines, founded in 1961, built various models in different sizes. The Pregnant Guppy was followed by the even-larger Super Guppy, with four Pratt & Whitney T-34P7 turboprop engines, the first example of which comprised components from the former Pan American Boeing 377 Clipper Constitution as well as the BOAC aircraft G-ALSB Champion and G-ALSC Centaurus. All the Super Guppy aircraft built for NASA and Airbus, however, were based on military Boeing C-97 fuselages, wings, and empennages. The first Aero Spacelines 377SG Super Guppy could be loaded and unloaded from the front after the complete nose, including the cockpit, was swung to the side. The first example, which differed in shape and power plants from the later Airbus aircraft, took off from Van Nuys, California, Aero Spacelines' base of operations, on August 31, 1965. Five more years were to pass before the further developed 377SGT version began its test program on August 24, 1970. After Airbus obtained its first example in 1971, in 1973 the European aircraft maker ordered production of another aircraft in the United States. So it remained at first, until after the ramping up of A300 production in 1978, the European maker identified the need for two additional Super Guppy aircraft and thus planned to double its fleet of transports. Aero Spacelines reached a license agreement with Airbus Industrie for the construction of two more SGT 201 transports, which were made for Airbus by UTA Industries in Paris Le Bourget. The first example, with the number "3" on its tail, was rolled out in May 1982 and was placed in service in August of that year with the registration F-GDSG. The fourth and last Super Guppy made flew for the first time on June 21, 1983, with the registration F-GEAI. The four aircraft were operated by Aéromaritime, which was set up by the airline UTA for this purpose with its base at Paris Le Bourget. Production of every single A300 and A310 required eight flights by the Super Guppy fleet, with a total flying time of forty-five hours during which they covered a distance of 8,000 miles. While Bremen and Hamburg (both MBB), Getafe near Madrid (CASA), and Nantes and St. Nazaire (both Aérospatiale) had their own company airfields and loading stations for the components produced there, the pairs of A300 wings, weighing about 22 tons, were shipped well packed from Broughton to the nearby Manchester airport by road, and there were placed onboard the Super Guppy. The first stop on the way to the final-assembly line was the MBB factory in Bremen, where the wings were completed with movable components made in other locations. Since a pair of fully functional wings would have exceeded the SGT 201's maximum payload, they had to be transported singly to Toulouse by Super Guppy.

Although the Super Guppy is difficult to control in turbulence and crosswinds, all the Airbus components transported by them reached their destination safely. This is true even after minor excursions into the green strips bordering the runways, after European storms took man and machine beyond their limits. Airbus owes its four Super Guppies no more and no less than its existence as a pan-European aircraft maker. Without its help, the gigantic logistics puzzle from the 1970s would never have been completed.

Since its replacement by the Airbus A300-600ST Beluga, examples of the Super Guppy at the Airbus factory in Hamburg-Finkenwerder and in the Aeroscope Aviation Museum in Toulouse-Blagnac are a reminder of this significant chapter in Airbus history.

It is a success story that continues at NASA. After its first Super Guppy 377SG was retired in 1990, in October 1997 it received the Aero Spacelines 377 SGT 201 Airbus Transporter 04 as compensation for the transport of two representatives of ESA, the European space agency, to the International Space Station. NASA's Super Guppy was still in active service with the American space agency in 2018. Its uses include transporting satellites or rocket components in support of space missions.

An aircraft with a big door. The entire nose could be swung to the side for loading and unloading. This was often a critical phase, especially in strong crosswinds.
NASA

A Super Guppy was still flying for the space agency in the summer of 2018, doing what it had been conceived to do in the 1960s: transporting large rocket sections. NASA

AIRBUS A300-600ST BELUGA

Beginning in 1995, five Belugas began replacing their Super Guppy forerunners on the high-density Airbus company routes between locations in Great Britain, Germany, France, and Spain. Operated by the Airbus subsidiary Airbus Transport International (ATI), the A300-600STs are based on the A300-600 production aircraft. Analogous to the Super Guppy, their fuselage shells are supplemented by the voluminous overhead superstructure, and the entire cockpit is lowered to the level of the subfloor cargo hold. The result is an enormous cargo hold with a volume of 49,440 cubic feet. If one compares the Beluga to the Antonov An-124, the cargo hold of the A300-600ST is 3.9 feet longer, 8.9 feet higher, and 2.3 feet wider than that of its Ukrainian counterpart. In June 1997, ATI established a world record, demonstrating that the Beluga is also suited for carriage of loads other than Airbus components. The largest piece of freight ever flown was a 43-ton chemical tank with the record dimensions of 58 feet in length and 21 feet in diameter, which was transported by Beluga from Clermont-Ferrand in central France to Le Havre on the Atlantic coast. Only the cargo hold of a "white whale" could accommodate this extraordinary piece of air freight. While air freight was four times as expensive as the alternative road transport, the result was carried out significantly faster and more safely than transport by flatbed the entire way.

In the 1990s, ATI tested the A300-600ST's suitability for commercial use in the market for transport of oversize loads with these and other spectacular flights. With a full load of 51.8 tons, in the early years a fully fueled Beluga could fly 1,035 miles. It was not until the fifth aircraft that the A300-600ST's fuel capacity increased by another 5.5 tons. The other four examples were modified to this standard in 2001. With its maximum takeoff weight raised to 176 tons, the Beluga was capable of qualifying for a crossing of the North Atlantic with a 33-ton payload.

The fact that the Beluga fleet still seldom operated on flights outside the Airbus consortium is primarily due to the success of the A320, A330, and A350 program, whose high production figures make all five A300-600STs indispensable on the company's routes.

AIRBUS A330-743L BELUGA XL

In November 2014, Airbus launched the Beluga XL program, which was conceived to replace the A300-600ST to secure the necessary transport capacities for the run-up of A350 XWB production and increased production rates in the A320 program. The Beluga XL is based on the Airbus A330-200 long-range jet and in the future will be the biggest aircraft to be operated on the pan-European traffic routes of the aircraft manufacturer. The lowered cockpit, the cargo-hold structure, and the vertical and horizontal tails give the aircraft a unique appearance, which at first glance resembles its direct ancestors of the whale family—however, on closer inspection it differs in numerous aerodynamic detail solutions, especially the tail section, which clearly differs from those of the earlier aircraft.

After the Beluga XL design was finalized in September 2015, assembly of components delivered from all over Europe began on the regular A330 final-assembly line. The lower fuselage segments, without the cockpit, wings, and undercarriage, were premounted so that the special aircraft being created was at least capable of being rolled a short distance. The actual transformation of the Beluga XL, however, happened in a separate production building on the Airbus factory grounds in Toulouse. The new transporter was first shown publicly on June 28, 2018, in the special Beluga XL paint scheme designed for it.

130 AIRBUS A300/310

Beluga world record: in June 1997 it transported a record-size 43-ton chemical tank from Clermont-Ferrand to Le Havre. *Airbus*

The first Beluga XL took off on its maiden flight on July 19, 2018. *Airbus / S. Ramadier*

On July 19, 2018, Airbus announced that the first of five planned Beluga XLs had landed at Toulouse-Blagnac at 14:41 local time after its maiden flight, which lasted four hours and eleven minutes. Captain Christophe Cail was in command of the flight. With him in the cockpit was copilot Bernardo Saez-Benito Hernandez and experimental flight engineer Jean Michael Pin. From their seats, experimental engineers Laurent Lapierre and Philippe Foucault monitored the aircraft's systems and performance in real time. With this premiere, the Beluga XL began its flight test program, scheduled to take up 600 flying hours in ten months, with the goal of type certification and service entry in 2019. The planned fleet of five aircraft is envisaged for transport of large aircraft components from eleven locations in the Airbus transportation system.

SPECIFICATIONS OF THE AIRBUS TRANSPORTS

Aero Spacelines 377SGT 201 Super Guppy

Manufacturer	Aero Spacelines, USA / UTA Industries, France
Number built	4
Wingspan	156 ft.
Length	144 ft.
Height	48.25 ft.
Power plants	4 x Allison 501-D-22e
Max. takeoff weight	85 tons
Max. payload	26.5 tons
Max. altitude	24,000 ft.
Cargo-hold volume	
Usable length	111 ft.
Length with constant height	32 ft.
Maximum width	25 ft.
Width of loading area	13 ft.

Airbus A300-600ST Beluga

Manufacturer	Airbus SAS, Toulouse, France
Number built	5
Wingspan	147 ft.
Length	184 ft.
Height	56.6 ft.
Power plants	2 x General Electric GE CF6-80C2A8
Cargo-hold volume	49,440 ft.^{3}
Max. takeoff weight	352,740 lbs.
Max. payload	103,617 lbs.
Max. altitude	35,000 ft.

Airbus A330-743XL Beluga XL

Manufacturer	Airbus SAS, Toulouse, France
Number ordered	5
Wingspan	198 ft.
Length	207 ft.
Height	62 ft.
Fuselage diameter	29 ft.
Load capacity	2 A350 wings (100 percent more than the A300-600ST)
Power plants	2 x Rolls-Royce Trent 700
Max. takeoff weight	500,449 lbs.
Max. payload	112,435 lbs.
Max. range	8,819 mi.
Planned service entry	2019

With its eye-catching paint scheme, the Beluga XL will be a future attraction at Airbus locations. *Airbus / S. Ramadier*

BelugaXL

AIRCRAFT DIMENSIONS

- Overall Length: **63.1 m**
- Height: **18.9 m**
- Fuselage diameter: **8.8 m**
- Wingspan: **60.3 m**
- Wing area: **361.6 m²**

- Launched in November 2014
- Based on A330-200 Freighter
- First Flight 19th July 2018
- Entry into service 2019

11 destinations

BASIC OPERATION DATA

Transport capacity: 2 A350 XWB wings (while current Beluga transports just one)

Range: 4,000 KM / 2200 nm at max payload (51 tonnes)

MTOW: 227 tonnes — Maximum take-off weight

Engines: Rolls Royce Trent 700

5 BelugaXL +30% extra transport capacity

© AIRBUS S.A.S. July 2018. All rights reserved. Design by Airbus Multi Media Support 20181754.

AIRBUS

An overview of the Beluga XL's performance data. *Airbus*

CHAPTER 12
THE AIRBUSES IN DETAIL
SPECIFICATIONS

Type	Wingspan	Length	Height	Fuselage Diameter	Wing Area	Wing Sweep	Power Plants	Max. Takeoff Weight	Passengers	Range	Crew
Airbus A300B (project state in 1969)	147 ft.	165 ft.	53.5 ft.	18.5 ft.	2,799 ft.²	28 deg.	2 x Rolls-Royce RB 207	138 tons	261	1,379 mi.	2 pilots, 1 flight engineer
Airbus A300B1	147.1 ft.	167 ft.	54.2 ft.	18.5 ft.	2,799 ft.²	28 deg.	2 x CF6-50	151 tons	320		2 pilots, 1 flight engineer
Airbus A300B	147.1 ft.	176 ft.	54.2 ft.	18.5 ft.	2,799 ft.²	28 deg.	*	A300B2: 156 tons A300B4: 181 tons	336	A300B2: 1,615 to 2,088 mi. A300B4: 2,983 to 3,666 mi.	2 pilots, 1 flight engineer
Airbus A310	144 ft.	153 ft.	51.9 ft.	18.5 ft.	2,357 ft.²	28 deg.	*	A310-200: 152.8 tons A310-300: 165 tons	280	A310-200: 4,350 mi. A310-300: 5,282 mi.	2 pilots
Airbus A300-600	147 ft.	177 ft.	54.2 ft.	18.5 ft.	2,799 ft.²	28 deg.	*	181 tons	345	3,666 mi.	2 pilots

*See "Engine Overview" on page 140.

The Airbus production center in Toulouse in the 1980s. *ETH-Bibliothek Zurich, Swissair*

The German air force's MRTT Multi Role Tanker Transports can be used for the transport of people and freight or for aerial refueling. *Airbus*

This A310 in the colorful livery of Uzbekistan Airways was photographed in the 1990s. The national airline of the former Soviet republic received the last A310 delivered by Airbus, construction number 706, in June 1998. *Airbus*

THE AIRBUSES IN DETAIL 139

The Lufthansa A300-600 in this photo is wearing the colors used by the German airline from 1968 until 1988. *Lufthansa*

ENGINE OVERVIEW
Engine Options Offered by Airbus for the A300 and A310

Airbus A300B1/B2/B4	Airbus A300-600R	Airbus A310-200	Airbus A310-300
General Electric CF6-50C2	General Electric CF6-80C2A1	General Electric CF6-80A1	General Electric CF6-80A3
Pratt & Whitney JT9D-59A	General Electric CF6-80C2A3	General Electric CF6-80A3	General Electric CF6-80C2A2
Pratt & Whitney JT9D-7R4H1	General Electric CF6-80C2A5	General Electric CF6-80C2A2	Pratt & Whitney JT9D-7R4E1
Rolls-Royce RB 211-424L	Pratt & Whitney JT9D-7R4H1	Pratt & Whitney JT9D-7R4D1	Pratt & Whitney Jt9D-7R4E3
	Pratt & Whitney PW 4156	Pratt & Whitney JT9D-7R4E1	Pratt & Whitney PW 4152
	Pratt & Whitney PW 4160	Pratt & Whitney JT9D-7R4E3	Pratt & Whitney PW 4152
		Pratt & Whitney PW 4150	

A Swissair A310 powered by Pratt & Whitney JT9D-7R4D1 engines, photographed during takeoff. *ETH-Bibliothek Zurich, Swissair*

THE AIRBUSES IN DETAIL 141

Evocative image of a Swissair A310 during takeoff. *ETH-Bibliothek Zurich, Swissair*

BIBLIOGRAPHY

- Facts, Hamburger Flugzeugbau GmbH, 1-68
- Facts, Hamburger Flugzeugbau GmbH, 4-71
- A300B, Airbus International, May 1969
- Press Releases MBB Hamburg Division, March 1971
- A300B, Airbus Industrie, spring 1970
- A300B, Airbus Industrie, 2/70
- Progress Report A300B, Airbus Industrie 3/71
- Progress Report A300B, Airbus Industrie 4/71
- The A300B European Airbus Program, Deutsche Airbus GmbH, 7/71
- Progress Report A300B, Airbus Industrie, 6/72
- *20 Years of Building Aircraft in Hamburg*, Werner Blohm, 1976
- *Introducing the SAS Airbus*, Scandinavian Airlines, 1980
- *Airbus*, Airbus Industrie, 1988
- *Airbus 89*, Deutsche Airbus GmbH, 1989
- *The New Lufthansa, 1955–2005*, Deutsche Lufthansa AG, 2005
- *The Time in Flight*, Premium Aerotec, 2010
- Airbus A300/310 Freighter Conversion, EADS EFW
- Airbus A300B4 Passenger to Freighter Conversion, British Aerospace Aviation Services
- Aircraft Engineering in Dresden, Daimler-Benz Aerospace Airbus
- *The Plants*, Deutsche Airbus GmbH
- Contemporary Documents, Company Archive Deutsche Lufthansa AG

THE AUTHOR
WOLFGANG BORGMANN

Wolfgang Borgmann's enthusiasm for aviation was passed on to him by his parents, who were active in the aviation field. In his early years he began building up an aviation historical collection that provides numerous rare photos and documents, as well as exciting background information for his books. Since April 2000, Borgmann has been active as an author and freelance aviation journalist.

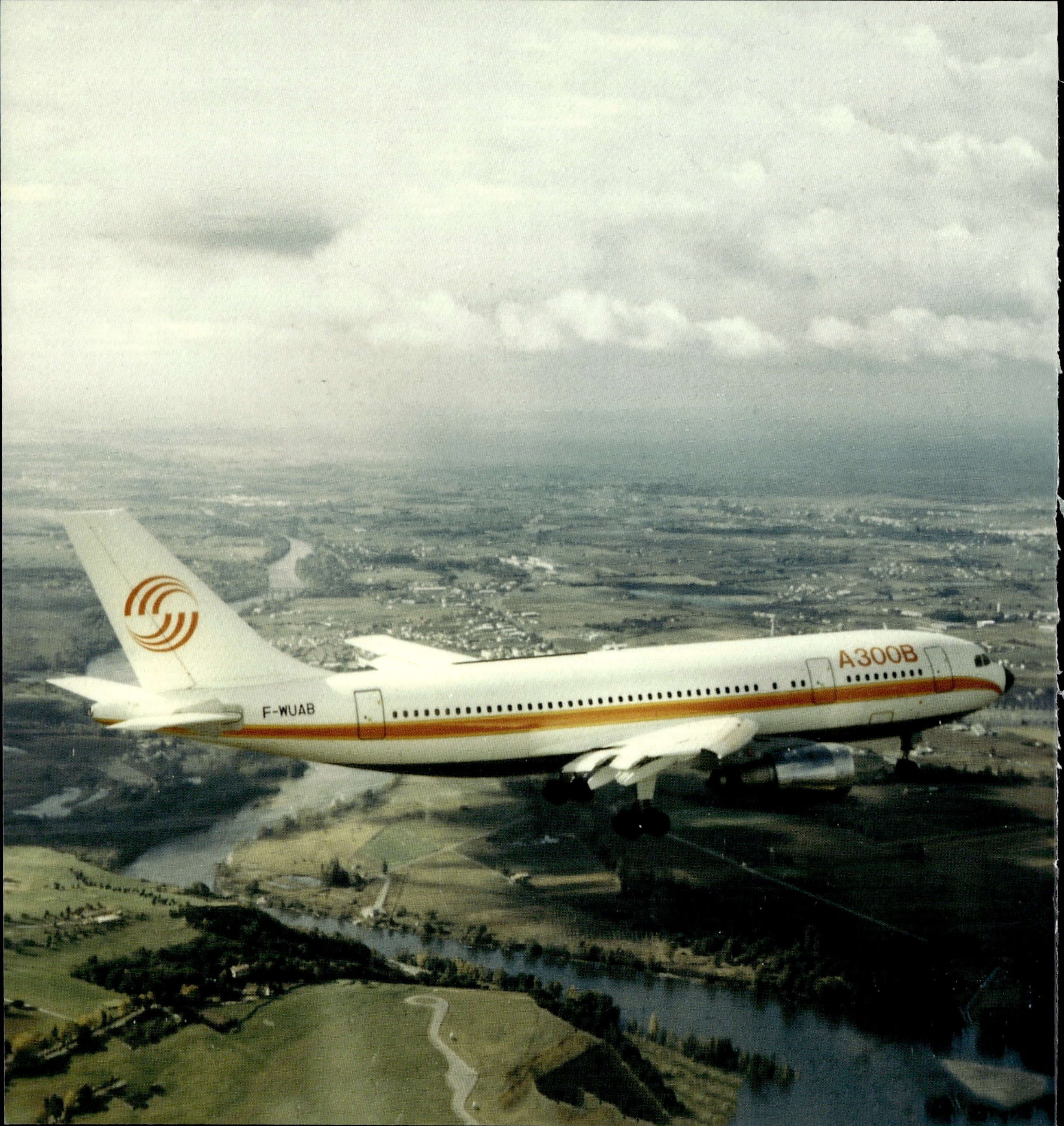
A300B
F-WUAB